The First-time Gardener

The First-time Gardener

Everything you need to make your garden grow

Published by
The Reader's Digest Association Limited
London ▪ New York ▪ Sydney ▪ Montreal

Contents

The best plants

Planting in containers

Maintaining a healthy garden

Introduction

Gardening can seem daunting if you have never had to get to grips with it before. But don't be put off – most jobs are simple, rewarding and fun. Tackle each task in turn, season by season, and soon you will be as good a gardener as any in the street, with a plot that repays you, your family and friends with pleasure and satisfaction.

The best way to start is to decide what you want from your garden – leisure, flowers, fruit, vegetables or a combination – and start planning accordingly. You need also to get to know something of your local conditions, such as climate and position, and how these might affect your projects. Then assess how much you can put into your plot – you will get much more enjoyment as a first-time gardener by being realistic about the time, effort and cost that you can devote to the job.

Once you have familiarised yourself with these basics, the secret of success is to know your soil, its type, what it contains and why it's so important for a flourishing plot. You need to learn how to cultivate it, improve its texture and make sure it contains all the essential ingredients for spectacular flowers and burgeoning food crops.

Techniques like planting, pruning, weeding, watering and composting are all straightforward and easily acquired from the relevant parts of this book. You will see that landscaping isn't the exclusive skill of the professional garden designer and contractor, and that a healthy, green lawn is within reach of the newest home gardener, not just the qualified greenkeeper.

Keep your eyes open for what pleases you in a garden, never be afraid to ask others for their own secrets of success, and you will have a garden to be proud of in no time.

Your garden

Why garden?

There are two kinds of gardener. There are the enthusiasts, who delight in producing minor miracles from the earth they cultivate, and there are the reluctant ones, who have to keep the outdoor space around their homes tidy – even though they would rather be doing something else.

Becoming a gardener

The enthusiastic gardener enjoys seeing seeds germinate, cuttings root, plants flourish, landscapes develop, flowers bloom and fruit and vegetables mature – and does not resent the amount of time that it takes to produce the desired results.

The reluctant gardener does not find tilling the soil such a desirable pastime, but realises that a certain amount of gardening is necessary in order to keep the exterior of the home looking reasonably respectable.

Fortunately, this type of reluctance often stems from a lack of experience rather than an unwillingness to grow plants. In fact, it is often converted into real enthusiasm, just by sowing a small lawn, planting a few shrubs and perennials or pulling the first home-grown carrots from the vegetable patch.

What is your garden for?

Gardening means different things to different people – colour, form, fragrance, food, wildlife, sound, recreation – and everyone who gardens gets satisfaction in his or her own way. When embarking on gardening for the first time, most of us have some idea of what we want from our plot, perhaps from visiting other gardens and seeing other gardeners work. Often, though, our first efforts are focused on keeping the garden tidy, and avoiding the disapproval of our gardening neighbours.

Keeping it simple

A garden does not need to be complicated to be pleasing. When maintenance time is tight, a neat lawn and well-planned shrubbery can look just as stunning as a garden stocked to the gatepost with unusual and elaborate features. Even a well-tended vegetable plot or fruit garden has its own orderly appeal. Above all, your garden is your own creation and, even if at the outset you take advice from friends and neighbours, television or radio gardening programmes and books on planning, your end result should be entirely personal. Few aspects of gardening are wholly right or wrong; two gardeners can have wildly conflicting ideas and techniques and still be equally successful. On the other hand, some methods are easier and produce better results than others – and who wants to make life difficult and get less than perfect results if a few simple tips can lead to an achievement to be proud of?

Gardening on a budget

Equally, you do not need to spend vast amounts of money to produce a striking garden. You might be tempted to rush to the nursery and fill the barrow with tools, plants and accessories. But taking a little time to write down how you see your garden, both today and in the future if you intend to stay where you are for the next few years, will not only save you unnecessary work but also a great deal of money. Growing from seeds and cuttings produces plants for a fraction of the price you would pay for larger specimens. More experienced friends will be only too pleased to pass on their surpluses, and car boot sales and local plant markets often yield amazing bargains as long as you know what you are looking for. The more you discover about this fascinating activity, the more your garden will be relaxing, exhilarating, satisfying and fun.

Guarantee success in the garden by planting bulbs. Put them in, forget about them and be rewarded with a show in spring. Perfect.

A garden for your needs

Your garden is the place where you and your family enjoy outdoor activities, and should be planned as such. You probably have an idea of what plants and features you like in other people's gardens – jot them down as a list and see if you can prioritise them in terms of need, cost and work required.

Important factors to consider include how much money you have to spend on the garden, how many free hours you want to devote to it – taking account of all the other pursuits and hobbies you enjoy in your spare time – and how good you are at putting your ideas into practice. You also need to look at your family's needs and think seriously about how long you intend to stay at this particular property. If it's your first home and you may be moving on in a short while, then there is not much point in planning elaborate features that take decades to mature. If you can achieve an attractive garden that works for you in a short time, then you will have the chance to enjoy it before moving elsewhere.

Food from the garden

Growing your own vegetables and fruit is becoming increasingly popular. You may want to set aside space for a small kitchen garden, or you may decide you can manage with a few raised beds and growing bags. Either way, this needs to be considered at the outset. And do not forget your shed – you will need somewhere to keep your tools, pots and other gardening paraphernalia as well as any overwintering half-hardy bulbs.

Entertaining and play space

Perhaps the most important consideration is friends and family. If you enjoy entertaining, you will need enough space to do this comfortably; and if you have a young family you need to accommodate them happily while indulging your own enthusiasms. If, for instance, you enjoy growing flowers but your children or grandchildren want to play ball games in the garden, you need to work out a way of keeping the activities separate.

There is no point in filling borders with expensive or precious plants and then wringing your hands when your budding Beckham and his pals use your flowerbeds as a goal mouth. Give energetic children their own area; if you decide to grass it, choose a hard-wearing variety – you can always turn it into a decent lawn once the kids get older. In the meantime, you can indulge your own passion for plants in your own space, unmolested by balls and boots.

Gardening with children

Encourage children who show an interest in the garden – many of today's best gardeners became hooked when they were children, helping grown-ups in the garden. Schools now actively encourage gardening as a part of the curriculum and it's a great idea to give children their own patch at home. Don't be tempted to relegate budding gardeners to an unusable corner, though, as their plants and seeds will be doomed right from the start – and all you will have done is give them a sense of failure and put them off for life.

A garden for animals

And don't forget your pets. It's possible to have dogs and cats and a decent garden, but there have to be compromises. You won't get a bowling green lawn if you have boisterous dogs, so think about having less lawn and more hard surfacing and shrub borders. Cats – all your neighbours' as well as your own – find clean, well-cultivated soil quite irresistible, a persuasive argument for ground-cover plants and a mulch of ornamental stone chippings.

A child's idea of heaven in summertime is the freedom to run around under a sprinkler on the lawn. The grass gets watered, too.

Discover your garden

The way your garden grows depends largely on two things – climate and weather. These vary greatly according to what part of the country you live in, and even in the local area where your garden is situated.

The period when plants are in active growth is called the growing season. The length of the season depends mainly on soil temperature, beginning when it reaches about 7°C and ending when it drops below this figure. The length of the day also has a great deal of influence – growth starts to slow down as the days shorten and nights lengthen.

There are plants for every situation, from drought-tolerant herbs and grasses (below) to shade-loving ferns and lilies (bottom).

Regional variations

The extreme southwest of England – Cornwall and the southern parts of Devon – has the longest growing season, which can be up to 360 days a year, while the Scottish Highlands has the shortest – as few as 150 days in colder years. The average for the rest of the United Kingdom is 250 days.

Higher average temperatures in recent years have meant that the growing season has lengthened by several days in many parts of the country and plants are sprouting and flowering considerably earlier.

Climate

General climate Four key factors – altitude, latitude, prevailing wind and proximity to the sea – affect the general climate. The south of the United Kingdom has a warmer climate than the north, so its gardens have a longer growing season. Gardens high in the Pennine Hills are colder than those lower down but at the same latitude. Coastal gardens in the west have a near sub-tropical climate thanks to the Gulf Stream, but in general all coastal gardens have a more equable climate because the sea prevents temperature peaks and troughs.

Local climate Here, the slope of the garden, its shade, soil type, shelter or lack of it and closeness to large areas of water all have an effect. A garden on a south-facing slope has a longer growing season than one on level ground, and particularly one facing north. Clay soil takes longer to warm up than a loamy, peaty or sandy one, but sandy soils can be more subject to frosts. If you want to extend the growing season of a particular patch of ground, you can help to warm it up by covering it with fleece, polythene or cloches for a few weeks before planting.

An exposed plot may be subject to battering and chilling winds, but shelter can cast shade, creating cooler pockets of ground. A large stretch of water nearby, such as a lake or reservoir, will have a cooling effect on hot days and may also affect local rainfall. A garden surrounded by high buildings or numerous tall trees may be in virtually total shade, with consequent reduced temperatures and light.

Microclimate This is the climate that exists in a small area – a garden, a border or even surrounding a single plant. Microclimates are created by many things. Walls, fences, hedges and plants will cast shade and reduce temperature and light; they can also cause a rain shadow and make nearby ground drier than in other parts of the garden. Frost pockets can occur if cold air is trapped by fences, hedges and other screens, especially at the base of a slope when the chilled air cannot escape to a lower level. On the other hand, screening the garden will also provide shelter from wind and scorching sunshine, and the heat retention of walls and buildings helps to keep the nearby air temperature a degree or two higher. If necessary, you can create your own microclimate by using temporary or permanent windbreaks, or cloches.

Weather

Rainfall Average rainfall varies considerably throughout the British Isles. The driest areas are in the east of England, the wettest are the Lake District and the mountains of Scotland and Wales.

All garden plants require a certain amount of water in order to thrive. So, if you live in one of the drier regions, for instance, it's a good idea to choose plants tolerant of such conditions as this will both improve the look of the garden and make life easier by reducing the necessity for regular watering.

The wettest time of the year is usually from October to January, but rainfall and dry spells have become much harder

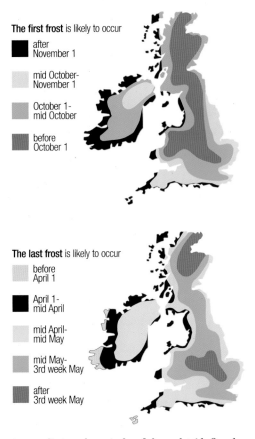

The first frost is likely to occur
- after November 1
- mid October–November 1
- October 1–mid October
- before October 1

The last frost is likely to occur
- before April 1
- April 1–mid April
- mid April–mid May
- mid May–3rd week May
- after 3rd week May

to predict and periods of drought (defined as 15 or more consecutive days without appreciable rainfall) are much more common. Snow can be beneficial to plants as it acts as a protective blanket, but most parts have seen a decrease in snowfall in recent years.

Frost This occurs when the temperature falls below 0°C. It harms certain plants because it freezes the sap in leaves and stems and ruptures cell walls. Furthermore, frozen water in the soil cannot be absorbed by roots, so during prolonged frost a plant can die from a shortage of water.

A late spring frost, when new growth has already started, is particularly damaging. If one is forecast, be prepared to cover up any plants that might suffer, using horticultural fleece or old net curtains. There's a good chance of frost from late autumn to early spring when the evening sky is clear and the wind is light.

Wind

A light breeze can be beneficial, blowing away old plant material and drying out waterlogged soil, but a gale, from any direction but especially from the north or east that has added wind-chill factor, can do tremendous damage, breaking branches, uprooting trees and bushes, and stripping young leaves from plants. A windbreak that filters the wind will bring enormous benefit, but avoid solid windbreaks as these create downdraughts on both sides that can flatten a planted border in a short time. It's therefore always best to choose a hedge rather than a wall for wind protection.

Temperature

Many plant functions – dormancy, seed germination, growth, flowering, ripening – depend on temperature, sometimes, though not always, connected to day length. Average temperatures are generally higher in the south and west of the United Kingdom, and lower at higher altitudes. Lately, average temperatures have been one or two degrees higher throughout the year, which has led to earlier springs, more prolific flowering and seed production and later onset of winter, and this change has affected all areas, enabling many plants to be grown outdoors that previously needed greenhouse protection during part or all of the year. High summer temperatures are not entirely beneficial as flower life is shortened, the soil dries out quickly and the germination of some seeds requiring cooler conditions is impaired. To be successful, a gardener needs to appreciate this, and all other aspects of the prevailing weather in the locality, right from the start.

In coastal places the sea has a tempering influence on climate and keeps wind temperatures higher than just a few miles inland. But you must choose garden plants that are tolerant of salt-laden winds.

Soil type and texture

You need to know what type of soil you are dealing with and its pH value (acidity/alkalinity), as this will affect how you cultivate the soil and the time of year you do it. Heavy clay soils are best worked in autumn before they become too wet, and sandy soils in late winter and spring. The pH will, to an extent, dictate the plants you can grow – you should avoid trying to grow acid-loving plants on chalky soil, for example. You can test your soil using a pH testing kit – these are available from most garden centres and DIY stores. It's a good idea to take samples from different areas of your garden as conditions often vary greatly from one part to another.

Sandy

Chalky

Peaty

Clay

Silty

- **Sandy soils** contain at least 70 per cent sand and gravel and no more than 15 per cent clay. The colour varies, depending on a soil's organic matter content. They are very free-draining and often lack fertility, but do have the advantage of warming up quickly in spring. They feel gritty when rubbed between finger and thumb.

- **Chalky soils** have a high concentration of chalk or limestone (which may even be visible on the surface as pieces of rock) and are often shallow, with a soil depth of less than 30cm over the rock below. They can be very fertile and are usually biologically active, with high populations of worms and beneficial bacteria. Chalky soils tend to be free-draining, but their high pH (alkalinity) limits the range of plants they can support.

- **Peaty soils** are more correctly termed 'organic', as a relatively high level of organic matter (minimum 15 per cent) influences their characteristics. They are good at retaining water and can be very fertile (unless they are pure peat). Although this type of soil is usually associated with plants that love acid conditions, there are, in fact, many alkaline organic soils. They feel loose, crumbly and fibrous when handled.

- **Clay soils** contain at least 45 per cent clay, and less than 40 per cent sand. Their high water-holding capacity means that they drain slowly; some are prone to waterlogging. Most are quite fertile and good at holding plant nutrients, but they can be heavy to dig and are often slow to warm up in spring. They have a smooth, soap-like texture when moistened and rubbed between finger and thumb.

- **Silty soils** are often referred to as loams. They contain at least 70 per cent silt with a clay content that is below 12 per cent. For most gardeners, these are the ideal soils, because they are usually good at holding water and are also free-draining, fertile, productive and far easier to work than most other types of soil. When they are moistened and rubbed between the finger and thumb they feel smooth but slightly gritty.

Garden features

Getting to know your garden from the start – what you want to keep or get rid of, and what you can picture there – is essential if you hope to get the best out of it, now and in the future. Take some time to think about these things and you will be well on the road to success.

Before doing any work on a garden, you should consider how much time you are willing to spend on it. Are you a budding enthusiast or someone who's only prepared to spare a couple of hours a week keeping it tidy? What will you use it for? Do you entertain a lot and enjoy having parties outside in summer? Do you have children who need plenty of space to run around and play ball games, or pets who may dig up new planting or scrabble the lawn? Do you like a formal look or something freer? How much space do you have available and how will your requirements fit into it? You need to consider all these aspects before proceeding with an existing garden, or when planning a new one from scratch.

Choose hard-wearing materials for a garden path. Gravel, stone slabs, bricks or cobbles look good – and will keep your feet dry.

Paths

A path should be smooth, level or gently sloping, wide enough for two people to pass each other comfortably, and without any unnecessary sharp curves or bends. It should be made of a material suitable for its purpose – if, for instance, it's going to be used for a wheelbarrow, then gravel may not be the best choice. Above all, any path must be safe – you don't want potholes, uneven bricks, slippery wood or algae.

The outdoor living area

This is where you may want to relax, barbecue or entertain. These areas are normally sited next to the house, but there may be good reasons for looking elsewhere. The part of the garden nearest the house might be in full shade or overlooked by neighbours. Wherever you choose, make the area big enough for all the activities you enjoy, and level and predominantly smooth so that garden furniture stands firm.

Enjoy the garden all year round, with a sheltered and inviting paved area – complete with comfortable seats and an open fire.

planning to consider. It's important for a wall to fit in aesthetically with the house, so be sure to choose materials that blend in. A wall will provide a sound and permanent support for climbing plants and, like a hedge, helps to block out traffic noise. Watch out, though, for any downdraughts that can damage plants close by.

The lawn

This helps to show off to best advantage other features such as specimen trees and flower borders, and is a useful overspill for your outdoor living area. A lawn can be time and energy consuming as it must be mowed and fed regularly in summer, though you may want to avoid moss or weedkillers for environmental reasons.

Make the most of a brick wall by adorning it with climbing colour.

Walls, fences and hedges

A hedge is generally planted along a boundary or to divide up the plot. Take care to choose the right subjects – if you want privacy, then look at taller species such as beech or laurel, but don't be tempted by rampant varieties, like the now notorious leylandii, that establish quickly but soon get out of hand. There are plenty of slower-growing shrubs that make an ideal hedge. Once mature, a hedge will need some regular maintenance – such as feeding and clipping – but it's an excellent way to attract birds and other wildlife into your garden.

A fence can do a similar job. It's less labour-intensive than a hedge, easier to erect and cheaper than a wall, and comes in many styles and colours – though remember a wooden fence won't last forever. A fence also makes a good support for climbing and trained shrubs, but you will need to access it from time to time for maintenance.

A wall can look magnificent, but the materials may be costly and a certain degree of skill is required for its construction. Furthermore, there may be local authority

Tuck in a small greenhouse so you can raise your own seedlings.

Beds and borders

Plants are generally more attractive when grouped together in a bed or border. The terms 'bed' and 'border' are both used interchangeably to refer to a piece of ground used for growing plants, but technically a bed is surrounded by lawn, paving or similar and is viewed from all sides, while a border is mainly viewed from the front and,

Careful planning and planting is needed to produce a herbaceous border as artlessly 'natural' looking as this one.

to a lesser extent, the sides. It used to be the case that different types of plants were given areas to themselves – for example, a rose bed, shrubbery, herbaceous border, formal bed of annuals, and so on. Nowadays this kind of specialisation can be impractical for space or maintenance reasons and most modern borders contain a mix of all types of plants, including annuals and bulbs, herbs and even salad leaves and vegetables.

Rockery

This is an area of gritty soil, usually, but not always, containing rocks positioned to simulate an alpine habitat. It's often used to edge a garden or to provide a dividing feature between different parts. The plants that tend to do best in the rockery are generally referred to as alpines. These include true alpines, which originated in mountain areas, and also dwarf perennials, heathers and shrubs.

A rock garden needs regular maintenance so that faster-growing plants don't swamp the slower ones. Frequent weeding is essential, especially at the start, as once

weeds become established, it's sometimes impossible to remove them without removing the rocks and starting again.

Trees

In a garden, trees are used either as shelter from the wind or shade from the sun, or to provide height within a planting scheme. Ornamental trees should be chosen with care as even those described as 'dwarf' or 'slow-growing' may eventually become too big for a small garden, and can cause structural damage if planted too close to the property or underground pipes.

If you have a very small plot, then it's worth looking at plants that are generally considered to be small shrubs – like bay, broom, fuchsia or spindle tree – trained to grow on a single stem. These are known as 'standard' shrubs and can be used instead of an ornamental tree where space is tight.

The kitchen garden

You may want to set aside an area for the cultivation of vegetables, fruit and herbs. With the upsurge of interest in organic

An orderly kitchen garden is as pretty as it is productive, with its ranks of colourful leaves and scarlet runner-bean flowers.

produce and television programmes telling us how to grow and cook our own produce, this type of gardening is on the increase. You can enjoy the fruits of your labours whatever the size of plot. With the help of plant breeders, who are constantly introducing mini-vegetable varieties that can be grown in tiny spaces, and dwarf versions of our most popular fruit trees, it's possible for many gardens to be largely self-supporting. You simply need to let your imagination run wild – so instead of a large veggie patch and regimented rows, make use of raised beds, pots, tubs and trellises – and add attractive edible plants to mixed borders, hanging baskets and windowboxes.

Greenhouse and coldframe

A greenhouse will allow you to raise a wide variety of plants from seeds and cuttings, overwinter half-hardy patio plants, grow tender plants that need the protection of glass for some or all of the year, and produce early fruit and vegetables. Heating your greenhouse increases the range of what you can grow, but can be expensive. Always position a greenhouse in the sunniest spot. A coldframe is useful for hardening off bedding and half-hardy vegetable plants and for certain types of propagation. If space is restricted, you may find you can manage with just a coldframe, and there are many 'hybrids' between a vertical coldframe and lean-to greenhouse.

The compost area

Every garden should have adequate means of composting green kitchen and garden waste, including leaves, weeds, vegetable peelings and waste crops, and there are many efficient compost bins on the market. Many local authorities now encourage home composting by providing free or heavily subsidised bins. Two bins are better than one, as one can finish maturing while you are filling the other.

The conventional place for the compost bin is in the vegetable garden. If you don't have a vegetable garden, site your bin in a sunny spot near the kitchen door, as well-made compost is sweet smelling and should not attract flies.

We have tried to avoid technical terms wherever possible throughout this book, but they are sometimes unavoidable. The definitions below put in plain English the terms that we have used, and give explanations of others that you may come across.

a **Alpine** Strictly speaking, any plant that is native to mountainous regions, growing between the tree line and permanent snow line. 'Alpine' is also loosely applied to any small plant suitable for growing in a rock garden.

Annual A plant that completes its life cycle in a single growing season – from seed to flowering, to setting seed and dying.

b **Biennial** A plant that takes two seasons to complete its life cycle – for example, the foxglove. In year one it forms leaves; in year two it forms flowers and seeds, then dies.

Bract A modified leaf which is sometimes brightly coloured and conspicuous to attract pollinating insects, such as the scarlet bracts of poinsettia (*Euphorbia pulcherrima*).

c **Chitting** Sprouting tubers, particularly potatoes and dahlias, before planting. The term is also applied to seeds germinated before sowing.

Chlorosis The loss or lack of chlorophyll – the green pigment in the cells of leaves and young stems. This causes the leaves to appear bleached and growth is affected – usually due to mineral deficiency, but viruses may be a cause.

Cloche Sheets of clear glass, rigid plastic or plastic film that are used for raising early crops in open ground, and for protecting plants from bad weather – alpines, for example.

Compost A mixture of loam, sand, peat, peat substitute, leaf-mould or other materials used for growing plants in containers. Also refers to organic material obtained by stacking plant remains such as vegetable trimmings, shredded prunings and grass mowings until they decompose.

Turning compost regularly keeps it smelling sweet.

Columnar or mat-forming conifers come in a range of colours.

Conifer Tree or shrub, usually evergreen and having narrow or needle-like leaves, and which usually bears its seeds in cones – hence the name.

Coppicing The cutting back of trees and shrubs close to the ground, often annually, to produce vigorous young shoots. In gardens it's usually done for decorative purposes – to encourage brightly coloured stems or large leaves to form.

Corm The underground storage organ of some plants, including crocuses and gladioli. Similar to a bulb, it consists of a swollen stem with a bud at the top which produces shoots and a new corm.

Crown The part of a herbaceous perennial at soil level from which roots and shoots grow.

Cultivar Cultivated variety: a variant of a plant produced in cultivation as opposed to one that occurs in the wild.

Cuttings Many woody plants can be propagated by taking cuttings. 'Semi-ripe' cuttings are sections of the current season's growth that have begun to firm. The base of the cutting is quite hard and woody and the tip is still soft.

d **Damping down** Watering the floor and benches of a greenhouse to create a humid atmosphere.

Deadhead sweet peas before pods mature to prolong flowering.

Deadheading Nipping off dead or faded flowerheads from a plant to prevent seeding and to encourage new flowers.
Dot plant An isolated or specimen plant – usually tall – in a formal flowerbed, to emphasise contrast in height or colour.
Drill A straight, narrow furrow, often created with the corner of a hoe, into which seeds are sown outdoors.

e **Ericaceous** A term used for plants that grow best in acid soil, such as ericas (heather). Also used to refer to lime-free compost used for growing ericaceous plants.
Eye Immature growth bud, such as the eyes of potato or dahlia tubers. The term is also used to describe the centre of a flower if it's different in colour from the petals.

f **F1 hybrid** Seeds obtained by crossing two pure-bred, closely related varieties which have been inbred for several generations. The plants tend to have an increased level of vigour and uniformity.

Feathered tree A young tree on which lateral shoots grow on the main stem. They are left on the tree until the trunk is fully established – about a year or two – and then removed.
Fertilisers Plant foods in concentrated form, classed as being organic (natural) or inorganic (artificial).
Floret Small individual flower that is part of a large head or cluster – as in lilac or cauliflower.

g **Germination** The initial stage of a plant's development from a seed. Germination periods vary: given the right conditions of temperature, moisture, light and oxygen, it may occur within days or take many weeks or months.
Grafting Propagating plants by joining a stem or bud of one plant to the root of another so they unite to form a new individual. It's widely used in cultivating fruit trees and roses.

h **Habit** The characteristic shape and growth form of a plant.
Half-hardy Frost-tender species of plants that can only be grown in the open reliably during summer – for example, canna and French and African marigolds. *See also* Tender.
Half-standard A tree or shrub, usually with a single stem growing 75cm-1.2m high before the head branches.
Hardening off The gradual adjusting of tender and half-hardy plants, grown under protection, to outside conditions. Plants can be placed in a coldframe in late spring, with air gradually admitted until the lights of the frame are left off entirely. If you don't have a coldframe, place plants in the open and cover with fleece or similar protection when the temperature drops more than a degree or two at night.
Hardy Plants that survive frosts in the open, year by year, anywhere in the British Isles.
Herbaceous Any plant that does not form a permanent woody stem. It commonly refers to perennials which die down in autumn and reappear the following spring.
Humus The dark-brown residue from the final breakdown of dead vegetable matter. Often used to describe partly decayed matter that is brown and crumbly, such as well-made compost or leaf-mould.
Hybrid The result of crossing two distinct varieties or, occasionally, genera. Hybrids may either display a blending of characteristics from each parent or favour one more than the other.

i **Inorganic** A chemical compound or fertiliser that does not contain carbon. The term is applied to synthetically produced fertilisers, although some naturally occurring plant nutrients have inorganic origins, as, for example, the mineral fertiliser rock phosphate.

j **Juvenile** Plants which have a distinct early phase, when either the habit, leaf shape or some other characteristic differs from those of the adult. Eucalyptus trees commonly bear first juvenile and, later, adult leaves.

Lateral A stem or shoot that branches off from a bud in the leaf axil of a larger stem.

Leader The main stem (or stems) of a tree or shrub that extends the existing branch system.

Leaf-mould Partially decayed dead leaves that have broken down to a brown, flaky condition resembling peat. Oak and beech leaves are the most suitable materials, though all tree leaves can be made into good leaf-mould.

Lime Calcium carbonate, a chemical used in horticulture, particularly to neutralise acid soils.

Loam A reasonably fertile soil that is neither wet and sticky, nor dry and sandy. It's moisture-retentive and contains a blend of clay, silt, sand and humus, and is rich in minerals.

Maiden A nursery term for a young grafted tree in the process of being trained. Applied particularly to one-year-old fruit trees.

A layer of mulch on a hanging basket helps to prevent water loss.

Mulch A layer of organic matter, such as decayed manure, leaf-mould, garden compost, straw or composted bark, which is spread on the soil around plants. A mulch conserves moisture in the soil, adds nutrients and suppresses weeds. The term is also used for inorganic material including gravel and black polythene sheeting.

Naturalising Growing plants, particularly bulbs, in simulated natural environments, such as grass or woodland conditions.

Node A stem joint, which is sometimes slightly swollen, from where young leaves and sideshoots arise.

Offset A young plant that arises naturally on the parent, as with many sorts of bulbs, or on short lateral stems, as with sempervivum (houseleek).

Opposite The arrangement of leaves in opposite pairs, as on privet and lilac.

Organic Any chemical compound containing carbon. The term is applied to substances derived from the decay of living organisms, such as garden compost. It's also applied to a style of gardening that rejects the use of synthetic chemicals and products.

Perlite Lightweight expanded volcanic rock in granular form, used in place of sand or grit to open up or lighten composts used for potting or cuttings.

pH A measure of acidity or alkalinity from 0 to 14; the lower numbers are acid, 7 is neutral, and above 7 alkaline.

Pinching out *see* Stopping.

Plunge To set a pot or any other plant container up to the rim in the soil, or in a special bed of peat, grit or sand.

Pollard A tree cut back to the main trunk and maintained in a bushy state by regular pruning at intervals.

Pollen Male cells of a plant contained in the anthers or pollen sacs.

Pollination The transference of pollen grains on to the stigma of a flower. This may occur naturally by gravity, wind or the action of insects, or can be done artificially by hand using a fine brush.

Pricking out The first planting out of seedlings or small-rooted cuttings. The resulting plantlets are later moved into larger pots, pans or trays, or set out into a nursery bed or into their growing position.

Resting period The period when a plant is either dormant or making little or no extension growth.

Rhizome A horizontal, creeping underground stem, which acts as a storage organ.

Rootstock A propagation term for a plant upon which another is grafted. The term also applies to the crown and root system of herbaceous perennials and suckering shrubs.

Rosette Ring of leaves that all arise at more or less the same point on the stem, often near the base.

Runner Prostrate stems, such as those produced by strawberry plants, which root at the nodes to form new plantlets.

Self-coloured A flower having a single uniform colour.

Self-fertile A plant, particularly a fruit tree, that does not need pollen from another plant to set seed and produce fruit.

Shrub A branched perennial plant with persistent woody stems.

Specimen plant Any plant, usually a tree or shrub, grown where it can be viewed from all angles, such as when planted in a lawn.

Spit The depth to which soil is dug with the full length of a spade or a fork – about 25-30cm.

Spore A minute dust-like body composed of a single cell, by which lower plants – such as ferns, fungi and mosses – reproduce. A spore gives rise to an intermediate generation upon which the sex organs appear and which eventually produce plantlets.

Spur A short lateral branchlet of a tree – particularly on apple and pear trees – which bears flower buds.

Spur A tubular outgrowth of a sepal or petal that produces nectar.

Sterile Plants that rarely or never set seed. Many double-flowered varieties are sterile, as the reproductive organs have become petals.

Stolon A stem which, on contact with moist soil, roots at the tip and forms a new plant – for example, the cane of a blackberry. The term may be incorrectly used to mean Runner.

Stool Often describing a tree or shrub which is maintained as a clump of young stems by annual or biennial pruning close to ground level.

Stooling A task carried out to provide young growth for propagation purposes, or to maintain a foliage or bark effect, such as the juvenile state of some eucalyptus and the red stems of dogwood (*Cornus alba*). Sometimes called 'coppicing'. The term also applies to crowns and rootstock of some herbaceous plants, such as chrysanthemum.

Pinching out the growing point encourages bushiness and buds.

Stopping Removing or pinching out the growing point of a stem, either to promote a branching habit or to induce flower buds.

Stratification A method of breaking the dormancy of seeds born in fleshy fruits of many hardy plants. The seeds are exposed to a period of low temperature prior to sowing.

Sub-shrub A low-growing shrub, or one with soft stems and a woody base, such as marguerites and some mature bedding geraniums (pelargoniums).

Succulent Plants with thick, fleshy, moisture-storing leaves or stems adapted to life under arid conditions. Cacti, with leafless stems swollen with water storage tissue, are examples.

Sucker A shoot that arises from below ground, usually from the roots of a plant – such as in roses or raspberries.

t Taproot The main anchoring root of a plant, particularly applied to trees.

Tender A term to describe any plant vulnerable to frost damage. *See also* Half-hardy.

Tendrils cling to supports so plants such as cucumbers can climb.

Tendril A modified stem or leaf that twines around supports, enabling certain plants, such as sweet peas, grapes, hops and passionflowers, to climb.

Toothed Teeth-like indentations, usually along the margins of leaves, also described as dentate.

Truss A term used to describe a cluster of flowers or fruits.

Tuber A thickened fleshy root, as on a dahlia, or an underground stem, such as a potato or Jerusalem artichoke, which serves as a storage organ, and as a means of surviving periods of cold or drought.

Tufa Soft limestone which, because of its ability to absorb and retain moisture, is often used in rock gardens or troughs, where small alpine plants are able to grow on it.

Tuft Bristly, sometimes mat-like, habit of growth, found particularly in alpine plants.

u Underplant To surround and interplant larger plants with smaller ones.

Undulate Leaf, sepal or petal margins that are wavy.

v Variegated Leaves – and sometimes petals – that are marked, spotted or otherwise decoratively patterned with a contrasting colour, most commonly cream or gold.

Vegetative Propagation by cuttings, division, layering or grafting, as distinct from propagation from seeds.

w Weeping Applied to a tree or shrub of pendulous habit, either natural, as in some species of willow, or artificially induced, as in weeping standard roses.

Jobs in the garden

Clearing and preparing

Good preparation when starting a new garden makes all the difference between a plot that is healthy, flourishing and easy to manage, and one that is a constant source of worry and effort. In the long run, it's easier to prepare the site properly at the outset than to skimp the job and regret it afterwards.

If you are moving into a new home, the builder may have done some basic landscaping. Sometimes this can be a way of covering up a multitude of sins to sell the property quickly, but there is little you can do about it until problems start to show up. You are better off taking on a plot that has had little or nothing done to it, because then you can do things properly from the start. Otherwise, consider removing any cosmetic work already in place and starting again.

An overgrown site

If the site is overgrown, cut down all weeds, brambles and self-sown bushes first so you can see what you have got. The quickest way to do this is to use a strimmer or a brushcutter, depending on the type of undergrowth you are dealing with. You can hire powerful petrol-driven versions of both tools, or you can ask a garden maintenance firm to take on the job for you – be sure to get a quote, first. This may expose rubbish, rubble and other items that need removing immediately. If there is more than your local recycling depot will accept, or you don't have suitable transport for taking it there, your best option is to hire a skip, which will take all this and the cut-down weeds as well. You can then achieve a clean site as and when you can fit the work in.

What to do with weeds

Ideally, you should let the weeds grow up again until they have made about 30cm of new growth; then they can be sprayed with glyphosate weedkiller. This will kill off all except the most persistent, which should be allowed to regrow again before giving them a second treatment. From spring to autumn, regrowth will be fairly rapid, but if you begin clearing the site in winter, it's best to wait until the weeds reappear in spring before doing any further work.

Preparing the soil

Once you are satisfied all perennial and established weeds have been killed, you can start working the soil. With a small plot, digging (page 48) is the best option. Work on a small area at a time, and don't over exert yourself, especially at the start if you are not used to strenuous gardening. You may find that weeds start growing again on the areas not under cultivation, but these will only be seedlings and will come out easily when you reach them. Alternatively, you could give another spray with glyphosate. Either way, in the short term they will not start to take over again.

Using a rotavator

To get a larger plot ready for turning into a new garden as quickly and efficiently as possible, you might consider rotavating it. You can hire a rotavator by the day from most tool-hire shops, and once you get the hang of it, you can cover a great deal of ground in a single day. Before you start make sure that the area is free of perennial weeds. Some – like bindweed, horsetail, couch grass, nettle and dock – can put down roots and make new plants from tiny pieces, so even a small patch could reinfest a large plot if it was chopped up and spread by the blades of the machine. Once you are satisfied that the weeds are under control and you have well-worked soil, you can start making your garden ideas a reality.

Digging the plot, whether by hand or machine, is the only way to break up the soil and create a blank canvas for your new garden.

A weed is any plant growing in the wrong place. Weeds are usually native plants, but rampant garden species can also be viewed as weeds if they get out of hand and begin crowding out more delicate specimens.

Weeds take plant foods from the soil and can harbour pests, diseases and disorders that may spread to other plants. Because of this, it's essential that you get rid of them as quickly as possible, before they become established.

Clearing weed-infested ground

Nettles, thistles, ground elder, couch grass and other perennial weeds are strong-growing plants that can often revive from the smallest fragment of root, as well as from dormant seeds in the soil. Clearing perennial weeds is a vital preliminary task when making or reclaiming a garden.

Clearing by hand

Digging out weeds by hand is hard work, but in most cases it's the most reliable method, provided you then hoe off or hand pull surviving weeds as they appear. Divide the ground into manageable areas and deal with each separately. Dig the ground to split up the matted roots, then carefully fork through the loosened soil, shaking the soil from each forkful and picking out the weeds. Pick all bits of weed from the surface. Work over the whole area in this way, then fork through lightly again to expose missed roots. If possible, allow two to three weeks for surviving weeds to regrow and be removed before sowing or planting.

Weeding in summer

Many weeds, particularly small annuals such as groundsel, bittercress and shepherd's purse, grow fast in hot summer weather. If allowed to flower, they scatter thousands of seeds in a few weeks. Hoe bare soil regularly, ideally while weed seedlings are

Hoeing is the best way to tackle annual weeds, but take care round the stems of established plants.

small and the soil is dry. Pull up large annual weeds before they flower and add them to the compost heap. Never leave weeds lying on the ground, where they may continue to ripen and shed seeds.

Always fork up perennial weeds while small or spot treat with a systemic weedkiller as soon as you notice them.

Using weedkillers

A systemic weedkiller such as glyphosate kills all plant parts, including the roots, and works best on young vigorous growth. Don't apply it during periods of prolonged drought or rain. In cold weather it will take longer to

Removing perennial weeds

There are several ways of tackling perennial weeds, none of them instantly successful, but you will find that persistence generally pays off.

1 Use a long, slim trowel to dig out the long tap root of perennial weeds like dandelion.

2 Paint the young leaves of perennials such as ground elder with a systemic weedkiller.

3 Spray large areas of established perennial weeds with a weedkiller such as glyphosate. Once the weeds have died, you can remove them and replant the ground.

work but will usually be effective eventually. Cut back the top growth and allow weeds to regrow to about 15cm high, then apply a solution of weedkiller according to the manufacturer's instructions. Leave until the foliage is dead and then dig in or fork out the remains of the growth. Allow time for any surviving roots to start growing again, and spray once more; some persistent weeds, such as ground elder, may need two to three applications.

Mulching

This method takes the longest time to work, but is effective and involves no chemicals. Mow the weeds as short as possible and then cover the ground with a light-excluding mulch such as black polythene, weighted down with bricks.

A weed-suppressing membrane not only keeps down weeds but helps to prevent moisture loss, too. Cut holes in it for your plants.

An established garden

You may have your own ideas about what you want from your garden, but if you are taking over someone else's efforts, it's best to wait a while and see what you already have, especially if you move in during winter, when nothing much seems to be happening.

It may be tempting for the beginner to call in a landscape gardener, but don't be in too much of a hurry. You could end up spending a lot of money in haste, only to regret it later – because as your knowledge grows you will begin to realise just how much you can do yourself.

If you wait to see what you already have, and then begin adapting it to reflect your own needs and tastes, your garden will come to feel more and more your own – even if it was started by someone else. If you rely on a paid outsider's influence, it may never feel that way.

Learn about your garden

Start by getting to know your plot. While you are doing this, you may need to do nothing except keep things tidy – lawn cut, beds weeded, vegetable patch turned over, hedges trimmed and so forth; don't immediately clear everything out. Few established gardens have no useful plants or features.

If the garden has been neglected, your first job will be to clear weeds from overgrown borders, and maybe cut back shrubs and trees that threaten to engulf their neighbours. If you have never tried pruning before, it's a good idea to get a friend or relative who enjoys gardening to work with you – incorrect cutting back can cause irreparable damage to some plants.

Unfamiliar plants

Find out the names of existing unfamiliar plants and what they do at other times of the year. Try not to take out too much permanent planting until you have given it a fair chance; once you get more competent, you may find you want to incorporate it into your own scheme. Established plants are a bonus for making a garden look mature; furthermore, you can spend a fortune on larger specimens at garden centres.

Don't do it all at once

Gradually, as you become more familiar with your plot, you will start to recognise what is worth keeping and what is not. Rather than trying to deal with the whole garden, tackle one area at a time. Remove plants that are badly diseased, dead or dying, those you don't like and those that have outgrown the garden. Repair paths, drives and sitting areas that you wish to retain: even if you decide to change the surfacing materials eventually, they should be perfectly usable in the meantime.

Adapting what you have

Although you may have your own ideas, you could find that by adapting these to what is already there, you can have a garden as good as, or even better than you had in mind. It may only take a few simple adjustments – such as altering the shape of the lawn, increasing or decreasing the size of a bed or border, introducing an ornamental tree or two to give extra height, erecting an ornamental arch over a path or exposing or hiding a good or bad view.

Putting on your own stamp

While you are making minor adjustments, keep your eyes open for things you like in gardens nearby. Spend time researching plants and other garden features at garden centres, nurseries and horticultural shows – but keep a tight rein on the purse strings until you know what direction your garden is going to take. It will save you a lot time, money and hard work in the long run.

For an instant transformation, use pots and containers to soften hard edges and introduce a splash of colour.

Grass grows best from turf or seed in moist but well-drained soil, so late spring or early autumn, when the soil is warm and moist, are the best times for a new lawn to establish rapidly. Good light is usually essential, although you can buy lawn mixtures that tolerate some shade.

Planning your lawn

The size and shape of the lawn depends on the size and style of your garden: sweeping curves suit an informal setting; straight lines are more formal. If you are planning narrow strips of grass, try to make these multiples of the cutting width of your mower. This will make mowing easier and give you a more even finish.

Whether grown from turf or seed, make a new lawn slightly larger than its ultimate planned size. This allows you to trim back the edges once the lawn is established to give a crisp outline.

Seed or turf?

Turf provides an instant effect, but it's much more expensive than seed, although seed takes longer to establish. The deciding factor tends to be how long you can wait – if you have young children or dogs, turf is more practical.

Preparing the ground

Mark out an area slightly larger than required. Prepare the ground thoroughly to avoid future problems (page 37). First, remove perennial weeds by digging the area at least 25cm deep, then forking out all roots and creeping stems. Badly weed-infested ground is best cleared by treating with a weedkiller containing glyphosate about three weeks before digging.

Lawns from turf

The topsoil needs to be prepared to give a fine, workable soil to a depth of 10-12cm. If you plan to turf only a small area, you can prepare it by hand using a spade, but if you are covering a large area, then hire a

Turfing a lawn

1 Start from one corner; lay the first row along a plank or garden line to get a straight edge. For a curved edge, use a hosepipe to define the border.
2 Lay the second row at right angles to the first to make staggered joints, and butt the turfs up close together.

3 Work from a wooden plank to protect the turf already laid and firm it gently into position.
4 After laying, work sieved soil into the surface, paying particular attention to the joints, to prevent drying out and shrinking. Try not to use the new lawn for six weeks and don't let it dry out.

rotavator. The lawn should be ready for use in about six weeks. Keep newly laid turf well watered; if it dries out it will shrink and lift.

Buying turf

Turfs are usually sold in sections 1m x 30cm, rolled along their length. Many of the more expensive turfs are reinforced with a biodegradable plastic mesh, so less soil is needed to hold the root structure together, and the turfs can be thinner and up to 2m in length. Turfs should ideally be laid within 24 hours of delivery. If you wait more than 48 hours, the grass may turn yellow or the turf dry out before being laid.

Sowing seed

A seeded lawn may be slow to establish but, when sown at the right time, the results are usually good. You can also choose a seed mix that suits your garden. Most mixtures are a blend of several species of grass that will grow well together and provide an even,

Keep the grass lush and green with regular light mowings.

Lawn seed mixtures

Fine ornamental lawns These lawns look lush and beautiful, but will not stand up to hard wear. Mow with a cylinder mower for a fine close finish, and one with a roller for stripes.
Sowing rate: 35-50g per square metre
Mowing height: 1-1.5cm

Lightly shaded lawns This is the best mix for lightly or partially shaded areas where the soil is moist; it's unsuitable for deep shade, dry soils or under evergreen trees.
Sowing rate: 35-50g per square metre
Mowing height: 1.5-2cm

Hard-wearing lawns This mix produces a tough, good-looking lawn, tolerant of heavy use.
Sowing rate: 25-35g per square metre
Mowing height: 1.5-2cm

dense coverage. Sowing rates vary, so check the instructions on the packet.

Tip Sow at a slightly higher rate than recommended to achieve a thicker-looking lawn in a shorter period, but don't sow too thickly as the new grass may get diseased.

Mowing new lawns

New lawns sown from seed early the previous autumn or in April will be ready for their first cut at the end of May, but only a very light topping with a sharp mower is required for the first two or three cuts. Use a mower with a roller to encourage the grass to thicken out.

The first three or four cuts of any new lawn should be made on a high blade setting. You can gradually lower the height of the cut, but never remove more than a third of the total length in a single cut.

Watering new lawns

Water all newly made lawns for at least 2-3 hours every three or five days if there is no significant rainfall. The best way to do this is to leave a seep hose gently trickling on the lawn, moving it every half hour.

Sowing a lawn

1 After digging thoroughly, use a garden fork to break up any compacted soil to improve drainage. Level the soil, then allow it to settle for about two weeks. Any emerging weeds can be hoed off or treated with glyphosate.

2 Rake the soil roughly level. Work in a base dressing of fertiliser applied at the rate of 150-200g per square metre.

3 Firm the soil by shuffling over the ground applying pressure with your heels. Rake the soil again and remove any stones.

4 To sow the seed evenly, mark out the area into 1 metre squares with canes and a string line. Weigh out enough seed for 1 square metre. Pour the seed into a plastic beaker and mark the level on the side. Use this measure to save weighing the seed every time.

5 For each square, sow half the seed in one direction and the remainder at right angles. Pour a manageable quantity into your hand at a time and scatter evenly.

6 When you have sown all the seed, lightly rake the entire area to incorporate the seed into the soil surface. Water well.

One of the first essentials in a garden is a hard-surfaced area where you can sit and enjoy a drink, play, eat and perhaps cook on the barbecue. This outdoor living room should be as large as you are able to make it, as nothing is worse than being squeezed up when eating or socialising.

Installing a deck or a patio can have almost as much impact on your home as building on a new room. Updating an old patio can also rejuvenate and open up the house, making it feel bigger and more flexible – and making you more keen to entertain your family and friends, especially during the summer months.

You have a basic choice of two types of surfacing – slabs, bricks or tiles of stone, concrete or reconstituted stone; and wooden decking. The first is permanent and easy to care for, with a huge choice of finishes, but takes time to lay. Decking has a finite life, even when regularly treated with preservative and cleaner, but is quick to construct and instantly ready for use.

Any austere effect of a large area of hard landscaping can be softened by the careful positioning of pots of flowers and permanent containers of plants like shrubs or conifers.

Decking

This popular surfacing consists of a framework of load-bearing timber joists to which boards, preferably grooved to reduce

Constructing a deck over paving or concrete

You will need: ■ measuring tape ■ pencil ■ panel or circular saw ■ 7.5x5cm timber joists ■ wood preservative ■ paintbrush ■ cordless drill with twist drill bits and screwdriver bits ■ decking screws ■ spirit level ■ 10cm masonry bolts ■ packing materials (pieces of wood or slate) ■ string line ■ decking boards.

1 Cut the timber into lengths to create the supporting framework. Brush cuts with preservative and butt together in position. Drill pilot holes, then secure each butt joint, using two 7.5cm screws. Fix joists and any transverse timber in place. Check the framework is square and level, with a slight fall for drainage.

2 If you need to secure the frame to a house wall, use 10cm masonry bolts.

3 Fix the transverse joints in position. Wedge packing material underneath any part of the frame that is unsupported.

slipperiness, are attached. The simplest type of deck is built over an existing area of level paving or concrete, with a very slight slope to assist drainage. The hard surfacing under the deck helps to prevent weeds growing and forcing their way through the boards.

All large DIY stores and builders' merchants stock decking materials – these should have been pressure treated with a preservative to extend the life of the timber.

Measuring up

To estimate the timber, measure the width and length of the area and plan the layout of the supporting framework on paper. You need to form a straight-sided frame round the perimeter and fix transverse joists across it – every 40cm if using 2.5cm boards or every 60cm for thicker boards. For joists over 3m long, fix transverse braces every 2m to prevent warping. Work out the number of joists to cover the area, and calculate the amount of timber you will need for the whole framework. For the decking boards, find out the width and length of the boards you are using, then calculate the number of boards you require. If in doubt, take a plan of the area to a builders' merchant and ask someone to work out what you need for the project.

4 Cut the first decking board to length and lay it in place along the supporting framework and transverse joints, aligning it with one long edge. To improve drainage and ensure even spacing between the boards, use nails or pieces of card to leave a 1-2mm gap between boards, removing and reusing them as you fix each board.

5 Drill two pilot holes through the board over every joist and every section of the outer framework. Use a string line to help you to align the screws across the deck's width. Screw the board to the joists and frame using 6cm screws. Cut the remaining boards and fix similarly.

6 You may have to cut the final board down in width to make it fit. Set a circular saw to match the width required. If cutting by hand, clamp the board to your workbench and tackle a metre at a time. Get someone to support the end of the board as you work. Fix in the same way.

7 After assembly, seal or stain, if required.

Constructing a patio from bricks and paving slabs

If the patio is to adjoin the house wall, the top should be at least 15cm below the damp-proof course, or surface moisture will cause damp problems within the property. Slope the patio away from the house so water doesn't collect against the wall.

You will need: ■ paving materials ■ string ■ wooden pegs ■ rammer or post ■ spirit level ■ heavy post or vibrating plate compacter (available from tool-hire companies) ■ hardcore or crushed stone ■ dry sand ■ straight-edged board or plank ■ spacers ■ mortar ■ brush ■ hammer or board and mallet ■ trowel.

3 Compact the hardcore with the vibrating plate compacter. Use a post to compact it in corners. Cover with an 8cm layer of dry sand and level, using a board or a plank with a straight edge.

1 Roughly mark out the area and strip off the lawn or surface debris within this. Dig out the soil to a depth of about 15cm, then compact the base with a rammer.

2 Cover the excavated area with a 10cm layer of hardcore or crushed stone, and level.

4 Starting in one corner, lay the first course of bricks and slabs against a straight-edged plank.

5 Lay on a damp mortar mix and tamp level, using a board and mallet or a hammer handle.

6 Bed the bricks and paving slabs. Check regularly using a spirit level.

8 When you have completed the whole area, brush off the excess sand and mortar. Leave the paved area for a day or two to settle before walking on it.

7 Continue laying the bricks and slabs until the whole area has been covered, checking at regular intervals for levels. Fill the joints with a dry mortar mix, brushed well into the cracks.

Putting up a new fence can improve the security and look of your property, and give you some added privacy. It also keeps children safely in the garden. Fences should only be erected on your own land – they must not cross any boundaries. Before starting work, discuss your plans with your neighbours.

A hefty fence provides privacy and doubles as a vertical planter.

Putting up a panel fence

This type of fencing, which is 'hung' between a series of posts, is the most common boundary screen. Panel fences are easy to put up and far less expensive than having walls built, and although they can look pretty raw and unattractive when first erected, they do gradually blend into the surroundings, especially if used to support climbers and wall shrubs. They can also be painted or stained.

Erecting a panel fence using metal post holders

You will need: ■ sledgehammer ■ canes or wooden pegs ■ garden line or string ■ post driver (or offcut of wood slightly smaller than the socket) ■ fence posts (use 2.5m posts for 2m panels) ■ metal post holder (use a 60cm post holder for fences up to 1.2m high, and a 75cm post holder for fences 2m high) ■ spirit level ■ fence panels ■ fence brackets ■ claw hammer or screwdriver ■ nails or screws ■ circular or panel saw ■ wooden post tops

1 Start by knocking a peg into the ground at each end of the intended line of the fence and stretch a string line between the two points.

2 Position the first post holder by driving the spike about 7-10cm into the ground. To do this, place the post driver or an offcut of wooden post into the socket at the top (to protect the metal socket), and hold a spirit level against the sides of the socket to check that the spike is upright. Adjust if

necessary using the handles on the post driver. Using a sledgehammer, hit the post driver or wooden offcut until the flat plate on the spike is resting on the ground.

3 Position the post inside the socket, knocking it into place with the sledgehammer. Use a spirit level held against adjacent faces to check that the post is vertical in both planes. Fix the post to the holder by driving several nails through the slots.

Before you begin, it's important to mark out the intended line of the fence with a garden line or string. This will help to ensure that you put up the fence exactly where you want it and that it runs in a straight line. When putting up a panel fence, fix posts one at a time, following the instructions below.

Wooden fence posts, even when treated with preservative, are likely to rot where they come in contact with the soil. For this reason the bases should be sunk in concrete or, as here, set in spiked metal post holders. If you concrete posts in place, a quarter of their length should be below ground.

Always measure accurately between the posts to ensure the panel fits before concreting or banging in the spikes.

Close-board fence panels come in several designs, including a style topped with trellis panels (below). Treated wooden post caps finish a fence off and help to shed water, preventing the wood from rotting.

6 Place the second post holder at the other end of the panel, mark its position, then slide out the panel before fixing the metal post holder in place and driving the post into it. Attach brackets to each side. Replace the panel and fix it to the brackets using screws or nails. Repeat these steps until the whole fence is in place.

4 Fix two metal brackets to the side of the fence post (inset), and slide the first panel into the brackets.

5 Rest the panel on bricks or slabs to hold it in place while you check for height and level before nailing it permanently to the brackets. (Alternatively, the panels can be fixed to the posts by hammering nails through the outer frame into the fence post.)

7 Use a string line and spirit level all along the fence to mark where to cut the posts; leave about 5cm above the top of the fence.

8 Saw each post to length and nail a wooden cap onto each cut post.

A path helps you to get easily from one part of the garden to another – without it a well-used walkway can end up a muddy mess. But it doesn't have to be merely functional – a well-designed path surfaced in an attractive material can add much to a garden's overall appearance.

Designing a path

Before starting to construct a path, take account of who will use it, for what purpose and how much it will cost. For instance, gravel is relatively inexpensive, easy to lay and fairly low maintenance, but if you intend to wheel barrows along it, or if wheelchairs or baby buggies are likely to run over it, gravel will be a difficult surface to negotiate.

A grass path is as easy to create and maintain as a lawn, but if it's likely to get a lot of use, it could get muddy in winter and be worn down to bare earth in summer. For most uses, some kind of hard, solid finish is the most practical.

The path should, in most instances, take the shortest route from A to B. Keep the design as simple as possible, avoiding sharp bends or curves that tempt the user to take a short cut, and make it wide enough for two people to pass, if necessary. Where the path crosses a lawn, an alternative is to sink stepping stones into the grass so the mower can cut over the top of them. This will reinforce the grass where it's walked on most, without taking up a lot of ground with hard landscaping.

Choosing a material

Apart from the practicalities outlined above, the material of which a garden path is made is mainly a personal choice. The advantages of gravel or stone chippings may be outweighed by their disadvantages – they are not the easiest finish to negotiate, they need regular weeding once the path has been down a while, and they can tread off

The surface finish of a path creates a garden's mood – whether sleek and stylish (below left) or with cottage-garden charm (below right).

Laying a path

All paths need a good foundation, and whether you decide on gravel or something more solid, the preparation is largely the same.

3 Add a 7.5cm layer of hardcore and ram this down firmly.

1 Dig a trench the width of the path, and the depth of the thickness of the surfacing material, plus 7.5cm for hardcore and 5cm for sand. For a gravel or concrete path the trench will not be as deep, as you don't need the layer of sand. The sides of the trench must be lined with shuttering boards if you are using concrete.

2 Ram the soil, then cover it with landscape membrane to prevent any deep-rooted weeds coming through. This will not prevent weeds forming in the cracks later on, but these will only be seedlings and can be easily removed or treated.

4 Add the gravel or concrete or, if you are using slabs or blocks, a 5cm layer of sand, well tamped down. Concrete shuttering is removed after a few days when the concrete is completely set.

5 If you use slabs or block paving, fill the cracks between them with a dry mortar mix, or brush soft (builders') sand between the blocks.

onto the surrounding garden. Timber paths are fashionable, but easily become slippery and have a finite life. Chipped bark should only be seen as a temporary measure as it needs regular topping up and birds throw it everywhere. Asphalt is hard wearing but is best laid by an expert, and its appearance lends itself more to driveways than paths.

In the majority of cases, a hard surface – concrete, slabs or blocks – is by far the most functional. Pattern imprint concrete has a more natural appearance than the somewhat bland concrete path, but has to be laid professionally.

Garden paths

- **Functional paths** Paths from garden gate to front door should take the shortest route if they are going to be used by casual visitors. They can be made to look more attractive by introducing gentle curves or by using a variety of paving materials.
- **Decorative paths** In large gardens a second path can be used to meander through the garden and provide easy access to each area. It can be a continuous 'snake' of paving or stepping stones, or a combination of both.

Pergolas may be large or small, simple or elaborate, sturdy or delicate. Used to cover a path or link two areas of the garden, they tend to become a focus and must be sited with care as well as being soundly built.

A dark green woodstain softens the appearance of new wood on this pergola, and beautifully complements the climbing roses.

An arch is, in simple terms, a feature that can be walked through. It can be plain or elaborate, and used to support plants or not. If you intend to use an arch as a plant support, don't make it too fancy as, after a year or two, little of it will be seen.

A pergola is usually built to cover a path, enticing you to explore or lead you to a focal point or a separate area of the garden. It can also be used to delineate a seating or eating area. Pergolas may be heavy or light, and formal or rustic in their appearance. Bear in mind that if the pergola is to support climbers, it should not be too flimsy.

Design tips

■ For a balanced appearance, plan the length so that the distance between each arch is the same as the width of the pergola.
■ A height of 2.2-2.5m under the roof beams, and an entrance width of 1.5m between posts, is the minimum for comfortable passage, especially if the pergola is covered with plants.
■ Err on the side of strength when choosing materials and dimensions, so the structure can withstand strong winds and the heavy weight of wet foliage.

Structural hints

■ For increased strength, reinforce all the joints with T-shaped or angle brackets.
■ Use a spirit level and plumb line for accurate positioning of posts and beams.
■ Posts can set up to 3m apart, but the greater the distance between them, the thicker both they and the bearers must be.

Planting on pergolas

For plants like roses that need regular tying, fix vertical wires to the posts or wrap wire netting around them. Direct twining plants towards the post by tying their stems to a short cane, stuck in the ground at an angle.

Building a timber pergola

A simple wooden pergola, sturdy enough to carry the weight of climbing plants, can be assembled from the instructions given here. You can personalise or embellish the basic design in a variety of ways.

You will need for a timber pergola 4m long x 2m wide x 2.2m high: ■ 10cm x 10cm timber, treated with preservative, as follows: 6 upright posts 2.7m long, 2 bearers (main beams) 4m long, 5 cross beams 2.2m long ■ 8cm screws ■ 20cm screws or carriage bolts ■ 6 metal post spikes ■ sledgehammer ■ spirit level ■ chisel ■ mallet ■ spanner ■ drill

1 Using short lengths of timber, mark positions for the posts, three on each side and spaced 1.5m apart each way.

2 Drive metal post spikes into the ground to support the squared timber uprights. Use a sledgehammer and protect the top of the spike with a wooden driver (which you can buy) or a suitably sized off-cut of timber.

3 Wedge the posts in the metal spikes and tighten the two bolts on either side to secure each one; check they are vertical.

4 Position a bearer along the tops of the posts on one side of the pergola, with an equal amount overhanging at each end. Using a spirit level, check that it's horizontal. Mark the position of three posts on the bearer and the two midway points between the posts.

5 Using a chisel and mallet, cut out five half-joints at these marks, 10cm wide and 5cm deep, to house the cross beams. Do the same for the other bearer. Mark and cut corresponding half-joints in the cross beams, again allowing for an equal overhang, about 15cm, at each end.

6 Set the bearers in position, together with the three cross beams that join them, over the tops of the posts. Drill through the joints and use 20cm screws or carriage bolts to fix them to the posts. Join the intervening two cross beams to the bearers with 8cm screws.

How to dig

Digging over vacant ground in flowerbeds and vegetable plots at least once a year is the best way to break up compacted soil and incorporate organic material. It lets air in, improves drainage and in turn allows for efficient root penetration and better plant health as a result.

Digging is the most effective way to prepare the soil for the next growing season. It also keeps the garden tidy by burying unwanted plant waste and weeds. However, when soil is being brought back into cultivation from a neglected state, it can also lead to the emergence of weeds, as dormant seeds will start to germinate once exposed to daylight.

If you intend to grow shallow-rooted plants, you may not need to dig deeper than about 30cm. The exceptions are if the soil is compacted or is heavy and badly drained.

Single digging

This cultivates the soil to the depth of a spade blade (called a spit), usually about 25-30cm deep and is concentrated in the area where most plant roots naturally grow, in the top 10-20cm of soil. Mark out the area using canes and string, and follow the steps opposite. Use your knees and keep your back as straight as you can when digging and lifting to avoid strain and injury.

Improving your soil

Bulky animal manures and composted plant waste provide some nutrients, but their main uses are improving soil structure, lightening heavy soils, and improving the moisture retention of light, quickly draining ones. They have low levels of nutrients compared with inorganic fertilisers, but as the organic matter rots, it produces organic acids that dissolve nutrients already in the soil, making them available to plants.

A healthy, fertile soil needs a biologically active community of different organisms, capable of releasing and recycling nutrients so that plants can feed. For this to happen, there must be a balance between the amounts of air in the soil (so that the beneficial organisms can live) and water (so that chemical changes can take place).

Apply manures, organic mulches or fertilisers so your plants gain maximum benefit, either just as growth starts or part-way through the growing cycle. Apply dry fertilisers to damp soil, as plants absorb nutrients in soluble form. Avoid over feeding with high concentrations as this can damage or even kill plants by burning their roots.

Conserving water in the soil

Adding organic matter to a light sandy soil can improve its water-holding capacity by 25 per cent in the first year and 60 per cent in the second year. It will also open up a clay soil, which tends to dry out and bake hard in summer, improving its water-holding capacity. Annual applications are essential to maintain these improvements.

An organic mulch will reduce surface evaporation and help to:
■ suppress weeds – the mulch needs to be at least 8cm deep to block out the light;
■ reduce moisture loss – the mulch needs to be at least 5cm deep;
■ improve soil fertility by encouraging high levels of biological activity.

For best results, spread mulches evenly over the soil, and leave them to work their way in. Don't dig them in, or decomposition will stop due to lack of oxygen.

Adding lime to heavy soil improves its structure and drainage. It also raises the pH and neutralises soil acidity. This helps plants, as many nutrients are more readily available when there is lime in the soil. Add lime after digging to ensure its even distribution. Apply only in small quantities to avoid the risk of over liming.

Single digging

You will need:

- garden line and canes to mark out a plot (optional)
- spade
- fork to loosen soil
- wheelbarrow

1 Dig the first trench to one spade width and one spade depth.

2 Place the soil from this trench in a wheelbarrow and take it to the far end of the plot – or place it in a corner of the plot. It will be used later to fill in the final trench.

3 Dig a second trench, adjacent to the first, and throw the soil from the second trench into the first. (You can put manure or garden compost in the bottom of the first trench, if you wish to improve the soil's texture.) Turn each block of soil upside down as you move it, so that the surface soil lands at the bottom of the trench. This helps to cover weeds and prevent new weed seeds from germinating.

4 Continue to dig trenches across the whole plot. When you get to the end, use the soil from the wheelbarrow to fill the last trench.

How, when and where you sow seeds depends on several factors, including what type of seeds you have and how many, whether they will germinate outdoors or need to be sown under glass, how many plants you want to end up with and what your growing conditions are.

Sowing seeds outdoors

For good results, an outdoor seedbed must be firm, moist and finely broken down to give a smooth, level surface. Dig heavy soil in autumn or winter to allow the weather to work on it over winter. Light, sandy soils can be left until spring. You don't need to add organic matter; if the soil is poor, rake in a balanced fertiliser.

Plants for outdoor sowing

The following plants are all hardy enough to be sown straight into the ground.

- Brompton stocks
- Candytuft
- Canterbury bells
- Clarkia
- Godetia
- Hellebore
- Love-in-a-mist
- Nasturtium
- Sunflower
- Wallflower
- Beetroot
- Carrots
- Lettuce
- Parsnips
- Peas
- Spinach

- Hardy annuals are usually sown in March and April, but some can be sown in autumn to give the young plants a quick start in spring. Seed packets advise on the best times for sowing.
- Hardy perennials are treated in the same way as hardy annuals, but if you collect seeds from your own plants sow them as soon as possible. Germination decreases with time, so sow old seed more thickly than fresh and don't use any seed that is more than two years old.
- Pelleted seeds, coated with clay or other material, are easier to handle but need to be kept moist until the seedlings appear. Primed, also called pregerminated, seed is available for plants that need higher germination temperatures.

Sowing seeds indoors

Plants which cannot survive in the open during frosty weather, such as half-hardy annuals, are first sown in pots in a greenhouse or indoors. You can use this technique to bring on early blooms or crops, too.

Sow the seeds between February and early April. You can buy them from a garden centre or seed catalogue or collect

Preparing the seedbed

1 In warm weather, when the soil is dry enough to walk on without sticking to your boots, hoe or lightly fork it over to a depth of 8cm. When the soil has dried out, tread it down firmly to break up lumps, then rake the surface to create a fine tilth (the particles should be small and evenly sized).

2 Prepare rows in the soil for sowing – running from north to south, if possible, so that the seedlings will receive the greatest amount of sunshine when they germinate. Space the rows according to the advice on the seed packet. Use the edge of a draw hoe (see page 63) to make shallow 'drills' (channels) about 1.5cm deep.

Sowing the seed

If the weather is dry, water the seedbed the day before sowing – not after sowing. Sow thinly to make it easier to thin later. Otherwise sow pinches of seeds at regular intervals according to the advice on the packet.

1 Mix very small seeds with fine sand to help to distribute them evenly. To control the seeds, dribble them from your hand between the folds in the skin.

2 To close the drills, use the back of a rake to pull the raised earth back over the seeds – working along the length of the rows, not across them.

3 Firm the soil down gently with the back of the rake. Be careful not to bury the seeds too deeply or to press the soil down too hard. As a rule of thumb, cover seeds with a depth of soil about twice their size. Sow some surplus seeds at the end of rows so that you can use them to fill gaps later.

them from your own plants. It's best to use plastic containers, as they are strong and easy to clean. Small seed trays or 13cm pots are usually most suitable. Scrub containers that have been used before in warm soapy water.

Plants for indoor sowing

These plants will do best if they are started off in a greenhouse or in the home.

- Begonia
- Bidens
- Cosmos
- Dahlia
- French marigold
- Busy lizzie
- Tobacco plant
- Pelargonium
- Petunia
- Scarlet sage

- Aubergine
- Basil
- Courgette
- Cucumber and gherkin
- Globe artichoke
- Pepper (sweet and chilli)
- Squash and gourd
- Tomatoes

Space large seeds, such as nasturtiums and sweet peas, individually at regular intervals in a tray, or sow two or three seeds in small pots and press them down into the compost.

Sowing seeds indoors

1 Fill the tray or pot with slightly moist seed compost. When sowing very fine seeds, first sprinkle a little finely sieved compost on the surface. Level the surface of soil in a seed tray with a straightedge. Compost in pots can be firmed by tamping the surface down with the bottom of another pot.

2 Sow seeds thinly and evenly. You will find it easier to distribute fine seeds evenly if you first mixed them with a little silver sand.

3 Cover the seeds with a thin layer of sifted compost or vermiculite – a layer of about the seeds' own depth is enough.

Some seeds should be left uncovered – very fine ones, such as begonias, lobelias and calceolarias, and those that need light to germinate, such as sinningias and streptocarpus.

4 Identify the contents of trays and pots with plastic labels. Stand containers in water to half their depth until the compost is wet.

5 Ideally, put containers in a heated coldframe or propagator at a temperature of 12-18°C. Alternatively, put the container in a polythene bag and fold it underneath. Stand it in a warm shady place, such as a shaded windowsill. For extra warmth put it in an airing cupboard, but check daily for germination and then immediately move it into the light.

6 Once seeds have germinated, turn the bag inside out every day to prevent drips. When growth is established, take off the cover and move into good light, but not direct sun.

Pricking out seedlings

1 Seedlings are ready to be 'pricked out' (planted out so that they are evenly spaced with gaps between them) when the first true leaves appear above the seed leaves. Fill a standard seed tray – about 33 x 20cm – with moist potting compost and mark out plant holes about 4cm apart with a pointed stick or pencil.

2 Gently lift out a small clump of seedlings, complete with the compost clinging to their roots, using a wooden ice lolly stick or the end of a plant label. Hold a seedling by a seed leaf –

not the stem, which is easily damaged – and gently tease it from the other seedlings.

3 Lower the seedling into a hole and gently firm the soil down around it so that it will not yield if gently tugged. When the tray is full, label it and water the seedlings with a fine-rosed watering can.

4 Put the trays in a greenhouse or coldframe, or on a shaded windowsill. Three days later, move them to a sunnier, but lightly shaded, position. Keep the compost moist.

Thinning outdoor seedlings

1 Pull up and discard surplus seedlings while pressing firmly with your fingers around seedlings to be retained, so they are not disturbed. Alternatively, chop out spare seedlings with a narrow onion hoe.

2 Always clear away and compost your thinnings as they can attract pests and diseases.

3 Thin outdoor annuals once again when they touch each other, this time spacing them at their recommended distance apart. Intermediate seedlings will be large enough to lift carefully with a kitchen fork or a seed label for transplanting elsewhere. Water well after thinning.

Whether your new plant comes in a container or has been bought with bare roots, use the correct planting technique to get it off to a healthy start. Container-grown plants are raised in pots or trays but have well-developed root systems; bare-rooted shrubs are grown in the open.

It's a good idea to dig over sites for new planting well beforehand, if you can, so that the ground has a month or two in which to settle. If you don't get the opportunity to prepare the planting area in advance, you can still plant immediately after digging individual sites.

Buying bedding plants

If you don't have the time or space to raise your own annuals from seed, you can buy young plants in containers during spring. Don't buy them too early unless you can keep them in a frost-free place until it's safe to plant them out.

Avoid leggy plants and yellowing foliage – signs that the plants have been growing too long and have exhausted their compost nutrients. Steer clear of trays with dry compost or masses of roots growing through the base. Choose compact, bushy plants, well spaced out and all the same size, with healthy looking foliage and plenty of buds, even the first open flowers. Water and feed them when you get home and plant out as soon as possible, or keep them in a warm (not hot) sheltered place until you are ready.

Preparing for planting a shrub or tree

■ Mark out a circle, about 1-1.2m across.
■ Lift any turf and fork out perennial weeds. Then dig the area to the depth of a spade blade and fork over the base, adding compost or well-rotted farmyard manure and any turf, grass side down.
■ Make a planting mixture of a bucketful of well-rotted manure or garden compost and 100g of bonemeal, and fork this into the heap of excavated topsoil.
■ Before planting the tree or shrub add enough of your planting mixture to raise the plant to the right depth.

Transplanting seedlings

1 Prick out seedlings sown in seedbeds or trays in late spring (page 53). If they have been growing well they will now need much more space to develop. Handle them carefully by the leaves, and gently tease them apart so that you don't damage their roots. If they really are entangled, put a clump of seedlings with their soil in a large bowl of water; they should be much easier to separate.

2 Sturdier seedlings can be moved straight to their final growing positions, but the smaller ones, like these, are best grown on in a spare seedbed outdoors until they are larger. They will respond well to a warm, sheltered, sunny position; make sure that they never dry out.

Planting spring bedding plants

1 Clear all weeds and prick over the surface with a fork to aerate the soil. Rake the soil level and clear of debris, then leave it for a few days to settle.

2 Plant the edging first, spacing these plants 15cm apart. Then plant the other bedding. Space plants closely, 20-23cm apart, because they will make little growth before flowering.

Planting a container-grown tree or shrub

Mark out the planting position and dig a hole large enough to allow for 10cm of planting mixture (see below left) beneath and all round the rootball.

1 Thoroughly water the plant and stand it in the hole to check its position before carefully removing the container.

2 Fill in around the rootball with planting mix, firming it as you go with your fists or a trowel handle, and level the surface.

3 For trees, position a stake on the lee side (the side away from the prevailing wind) and drive it in at an angle of 45 degrees to avoid damaging the rootball. Secure the tree with an adjustable tie.

Check plants before buying

- Avoid bare-root plants with shrivelled or discoloured stems or buds beginning to grow, or that have white hair-roots appearing.
- Distorted stems may indicate a diseased or badly grown plant.
- If the soil around the roots of a rootballed plant is held together with netting and you want to check the condition, squeeze the rootball between your hands. It should be firm and moist. If the mesh is damaged or the soil too loosely packed, the roots may have started to dry out.

Planting bare-root trees and shrubs

Bare-rooted trees and shrubs are ordered from a nursery in advance and delivered between November and March. They should be planted as soon as possible after delivery, but not when the ground is frozen.

1 Before planting, tidy and trim plants to size. Prune each stem back to three to five buds long (climbers and ramblers to about 1.2m) and remove any dead wood and weak growth. Trim 5-8cm off the end of each main root.

2 After placing the plant in the prepared site, check that the plant is at its original depth; in the case of a rose, make sure the bud joint (the bulge immediately above the roots) is just below surface level. The hole should be large enough to take the roots comfortably when they are evenly spread out over a small mound of soil.

3 Carefully replace the excavated soil over the roots, a little at a time, shaking the plant from time to time to ensure soil fills all air pockets between the roots.

4 When the hole is completely filled, firm all round the plant using your hands or feet, and level the surface.

How to move an established shrub

Shrubs – deciduous or evergreen – can be moved to a new part of the garden in autumn or spring, but not when the soil is frozen or waterlogged. Small, young shrubs transplant more easily than larger, well-established ones. Prepare a hole about 1m across and 45cm deep in the new site.

1 Use a spade to mark a circle 60-75cm in diameter around the plant to be moved. Tie up arching branches with string.

2 Dig a trench one spade blade deep outside the circle. With a fork loosen some of the soil from the fibrous roots to reduce the weight of the rootball.

3 Undercut the rootball by digging down at an angle, slicing through woody roots. Work round until the rootball is free. Check that the new hole you have dug is big enough, and adjust it if necessary.

4 If the plant is large and heavy, enlist a helper. Tilt the plant to one side and ease a piece of strong sacking or plastic sheet underneath. Lean the plant the opposite way and pull the sheet through.

5 Tie up the sheet securely to keep the rootball intact, and lift or drag the plant on the sheet to its new home. Plant at the same depth as before, firm in, water well and mulch.

Gather up your garden and kitchen waste and recycle it to provide a free supply of nutrients for the garden. Composting is not difficult or smelly – it's a means of speeding up the natural process of decomposition.

Making compost

The secret of making good compost is to mix quick-rotting green waste and tougher fibrous materials in roughly equal amounts, and keep them warm and moist in a lidded container, preferably insulated to prevent heat loss. Add a mixture of materials in 15cm layers or fork them into the heap. Shred woody waste or cut into small pieces. Large quantities of grass cuttings will not go slimy or smelly if mixed with torn crumpled paper or egg boxes, while fibrous waste will rot faster mixed with grass cuttings and similar green material.

■ Continue to add waste until the container is full, although the level will sink as the contents rot.

■ Check that the materials are moist; water occasionally in hot weather.

■ Cover the top with an old blanket, piece of carpet or a layer of straw if there is no lid, and leave to rot for at least six months in summer – rotting will tend to slow down over winter.

Compost ingredients

Quick-rotting materials

■ Soft, sappy, green waste such as weeds, young plants, soft (not woody) prunings, fruit, and raw fruit and vegetable peelings.

■ Lawn cuttings and nettles.

■ Horse and poultry manure, tea and coffee grounds (including tea bags and filter papers), and used pet litter such as hay from rabbits, guinea pigs and pigeons.

Slow-rotting materials

■ Fibrous materials such as shredded paper and card products, straw, vegetable stems, leaves, eggshells and soft hedge prunings.

In six to twelve months, raw kitchen and garden waste (top) will have rotted down into a crumbly mass at the bottom of the compost bin (above) – a valuable and free source of organic matter.

■ Shredded or chopped thick stems and woody material.

■ Don't use: meat and fish scraps; cat and dog faeces; plastic and synthetic fibres; coal ash; wood, metal or glass; diseased plant material; perennial and seeding weeds.

Starting with composting

A ready-made compost bin is the easiest way to get started with compost. They come in all shapes and sizes and most work reasonably well, but some designs make better and quicker compost than others. They also range widely in price – where cost is the main factor, try contacting your local authority, as most offer either free or heavily subsidised compost bins.

■ A round bin takes up more unproductive space than a square or rectangular one. Several square bins can be positioned side by side and will keep each other warm.

■ Dark colours absorb heat more readily, so organic materials break down quicker.

■ The ingredients in the centre heat up and stay hot more efficiently than those around the edge, so the larger the bin, the more efficient it is.

■ Ensure there is an easy way of extracting the compost when it's ready. Inexpensive, round bins are usually bigger at the bottom than the top, so can be slid up to access the compost; more expensive ones should have a door somewhere near the base.

■ The thicker the walls, the hotter the compost will get. Thin plastic will cool off when the outside temperature drops. Wood is a good insulator, but rots in time. Some bins are made of twin-wall plastic sheets, which work in a similar way to double glazing and produce compost more quickly.

■ Make sure the bin has a well-fitting lid. There is no need for the bin to have air holes as enough air is introduced every time you add materials.

You can make compost in every garden, whether in a small, collapsible plastic bin (above) or big, wooden bins that you can make from a kit. If you have two bins, you can fill one as the other matures.

The right tool for the job

A few basic tools will enable you to accomplish most garden tasks, but some extra items designed for particular jobs will add versatility to your tool kit. You may also want to try out a few more specialised pieces of equipment, some of which you may eventually find indispensable.

Cultivation tools

Always buy the best tools you can afford. Stainless-steel versions are much cheaper than they used to be and are easier both to use and to clean.

Spades, forks and rakes

■ **Spade** Used primarily for digging, making planting holes and moving or mixing soil, a spade is also useful for skimming off weeds, tidying border edges and mixing compost. The blade is attached to a wooden or metal shaft fitted with a plastic or wooden D or T-shaped handle. In a good-quality spade, the blade and tubular neck are forged from a single piece of metal for strength, and the blade has a tread on the top edge which makes digging easier on the feet. Standard spades have a 28 x 19cm blade and a 70cm-73cm shaft, but for taller gardeners a 98cm shaft is available. A border spade has a smaller blade – 23 x 13cm – and is designed for working in small spaces or where a lighter model is easier to use.

The familiar design of basic gardening tools – fork, spade, hoe and rake – has changed little since our grandfathers' days.

Using a spade or fork

■ Keep your back straight.

■ Insert the full head of the spade or fork vertically into the soil to its maximum depth.

■ When lifting soil or plants, steady the handle with one hand and move the other close to the head.

■ Clean the head regularly during use by plunging it into a bucket of sand or scraping it with a flat piece of wood or a paint scraper.

■ **Fork** A garden fork is used for general cultivation work, such as breaking down soil after digging, pricking over and loosening the surface. It can also be used for lifting root vegetables, and for moving plants and bulky manure. Most forks have four metal prongs, or tines, forged from a single piece of metal. They are fitted with the same kinds of shafts and handles as spades. On a standard fork, the tines are 30cm long and the head is 20cm wide, but a border fork has smaller tines and is narrower (23 x 14cm).

■ **Rake** A soil rake is used for levelling and surface preparation, especially when making a seedbed. The long wooden or plastic-covered metal shaft should allow you to stand upright while raking to reduce back strain – 1.5m is comfortable for most gardeners. The shaft is attached to a steel head fitted with forged steel tines. As you move the head backwards and forwards over soil, the tines loosen the surface and break up lumps as you level the ground. Held in a more upright position, a rake can be used to comb stones and weeds across the surface. Once you have prepared a seedbed, you can turn the rake over and use a corner to draw out a drill for sowing. A spring-tined rake is useful for clearing up leaves and raking thatch out of the garden.

A dutch hoe is ideal for getting rid of young weeds (above). The draw hoe's angled head will chop off weeds as it moves forwards.

Hoes

There are two basic types of long-handled hoe – dutch hoes, which skim the soil surface when pushed away from you, and draw hoes, which do the same when pulled towards you. In each case, walk backwards to avoid treading on the area you have hoed.

■ **Dutch hoe** The flat blade is attached to a long handle at a slight angle. To loosen soil and destroy weeds, push the hoe to and fro, with the blade just below the surface.

■ **Draw hoe** The rectangular head, joined to the handle at a right angle, chops out weeds and breaks up the surface while moving towards you. It is also good for scraping off stones and earthing up potatoes.

■ **Swoe cultivator** This useful angled hoe looks a bit like a golf club. Its sharp-edged blade slides under the soil backwards, forwards or at an angle, and if you turn it on its edge, you can use the point to create neat seed drills or to dig small planting holes.

A one-piece head is stronger than a riveted one; 12 tines are enough for smaller plots but go for 16 or more for larger areas.

Hand tools

■ **Hand cultivator** This is used to loosen and aerate soil between plants and in spaces where a hoe cannot reach.

■ **Trowel** Used for surface cultivation and measuring small amounts of soil, compost or fertiliser – buy the best you can afford.

A hand cultivator (above) doubles as a rake or a hoe in small spaces; a good trowel is an essential piece of gardening equipment.

■ **Hand fork** Of similar construction and size to a trowel, this has three or four flattened tines and is used for weeding in confined spaces, lifting young plants and lightly cultivating small areas.

Pruning and maintenance tools

Secateurs and loppers

■ **Bypass secateurs** They work with a scissors action, and are used for most kinds of pruning, deadheading and trimming.

■ **Anvil secateurs** A single sharp blade cuts against a flat surface.

■ **Loppers** Long-handled pruners will cut stems up to about 2.5cm in diameter. They

Sharp secateurs are vital if you have a lot of woody shrubs to prune; choose from bypass or 'parrot beak' (left) or anvil (right).

are fitted with anvil or bypass secateur heads, often with a ratchet to reduce the effort needed to cut hard, thick stems.

■ **Tree loppers or long-arm pruners** The cutting heads are on the end of fixed or extending poles up to 5m long.

Saws

■ **Pruning saw** Use a fixed or folding pruning saw to cut branches thicker than 2.5cm in diameter. The saw is designed to access confined places between branches.

■ **Bow saw** This blade, tensioned in a bent tubular handle, is used for larger branches.

Shears

■ **Garden shears** Used to trim hedges, shrubs and small areas of grass. Straight-edged kinds are easy to sharpen and maintain; those with wavy cutting edges are good for cutting thicker stems. Some have long or extending handles for greater reach.

Hedge trimming is easy with sharp garden shears.

Watering can roses are available in a range of different sizes.

Watering equipment

■ **Hosepipes** The best hosepipes are reinforced with nylon, which prevents kinking and increases life. You also need a tap connector and possibly a spray nozzle for the other end. A wall-mounted reel is convenient for storing; one on wheels is useful for moving the hose around.

■ **Watering can** Choose a 9 litre model for general garden work and a 4.5 litre one for the greenhouse, coldframe and conservatory. A fine rose is used for watering seeds and seedlings, a coarse one for general watering.

■ **Mister** Useful for misting cuttings and young plants, and applying foliar feeds and small amounts of liquid chemicals.

Caring for tools

Tools that are regularly cleaned and neatly stored are always ready for use.

■ Allocate storage space for each tool where it's accessible and cannot be damaged.

■ Clean all tools after use. Scrape or brush off debris, wipe metal blades with an oily rag to prevent rust, and grease metal parts.

■ Keep cutting tools sharp. Pruning equipment needs regular honing to keep it sharp so that it cuts without damaging the plant, and without undue effort. Spade and hoe blades are also easier to use if you sometimes file their edges sharp.

Good-quality carrying equipment will make gardening less tiring. A wheelbarrow and watering can are essential; a rubber trug-bucket, metal pail, plastic carrying sheet and bags are useful extras.

■ **One-handed shears** Sprung to open automatically, these are useful for light trimming, deadheading and for cutting small areas of grass. They may be fitted with swivelling blades to adjust the angle of cut.

Carrying equipment

■ **Bucket** Useful for carrying and watering.

■ **Carrying sheets and bags** Made of tear-proof woven plastic, carrying sheets and bags are useful for tidying the garden and for carrying prunings, trimmings and weeds. They are light and easily stored.

■ **Wheelbarrow** Used to transport heavy materials such as soil, compost and larger tools. It's usually fitted with a single wheel; a pneumatic tyre rather than a solid one is easier for wheeling over long distance.

Garden machinery

Although powered garden machinery is not absolutely essential for keeping the garden in good heart, it can save time and reduce hard work to turn to powered tools if you have a larger garden or maintenance time is at a premium.

Lawnmowers, see page 108

Cutting tools

As well as lawnmowers, a number of other tools are available for specific trimming jobs around lawn edges and for awkward places where a mower cannot be used.

■ **Spin trimmers** Light, hand-held machines that are useful for trimming long grass around trees or in difficult corners. Powered by a petrol engine or electricity, they cut using a length of nylon cord rotating horizontally at high speed or a sharp blade for brushwood cutting.

■ **Powered hedge-trimmers** An electric or petrol-powered hedge-trimmer can save time and effort if you have a large hedge. With either single or double-sided

A leaf blower makes short work of tidying the autumn garden.

reciprocating blades, these machines require great care during use. Always keep power cables safely out of the way, and use a circuit breaker. Wear thick gloves, goggles and ear defenders.

■ **Chainsaws** These have become more popular for the home gardener since the prices have fallen to a more affordable level. They are powered either by petrol or electricity – electrically powered ones are lighter but can only be used near an accessible power supply. These tools need operating with great care, and full protective clothing and goggles must be worn. For single jobs requiring a chainsaw, it's usually better to call in a professional contractor, making sure the firm has full liability insurance. Curiously enough, anyone can buy a chainsaw, but you are only allowed to hire one from a tool-hire company if you can produce a certificate of operation proficiency.

■ **Leaf blower or vacuum** A hand-held machine with a strong fan powered by a two-stroke petrol engine or mains electricity. It blows leaves and debris into one area or sucks them into a chamber or bag. A push-along leaf sweeper collects leaves, debris and dead grass but is not effective when leaves and grass are wet.

A powerful chainsaw requires expert handling to avoid injury.

Sprinklers

A sprinkler, attached to the end of a hosepipe, is useful for watering a large area of garden.

■ **Static sprinklers** spray a circular area.

■ **Oscillating sprinklers** revolve or swing from side to side and cover a wide area; the reach is adjustable.

■ **Travelling sprinklers** creep slowly across the lawn or other smooth, level piece of ground, powered by the water flow.

Cultivating a large area

Petrol-powered rotavators or cultivators are excellent for tilling a larger garden, turning in weeds and mixing in manure or compost. Attachments are available for earthing up, making seedbeds and tilling between crops. Most machines can be set to work at different depths and some have adjustable handles, allowing you to walk to one side on uncultivated soil. Buy a sturdy, easily managed model, suited to the size of the garden, and maintain it regularly, or hire an appropriate type and cultivate as much ground as possible in one go.

A rotating pulse jet sprinkler needs moving at intervals; the fountain created by a swing sprinkler covers a wide area of lawn.

The
best
plants

Plants come in all shapes, sizes and kinds. Choosing the right ones not only makes for a beautiful and thriving garden, but will save you time, money and disappointment in the long run.

Plants for a purpose

Trees and shrubs
Woody plants are the backbone of any garden, whatever the size. They give height and form, and range from shrubs a few centimetres high to trees of several metres height and spread.

■ **Evergreens** shed their oldest leaves a few at a time throughout the year, so are fully clothed all year round. They include laurels and hollies, and most conifers – which are trees and shrubs that bear cones and have needle-like leaves. Evergreens, particularly those with foliage other than green, are useful for giving a garden colour in winter,

The structure of the garden is defined not only by its hard landscaping, but also by its planting – of trees, shrubs and climbers on supports.

but plant too many and you can end up making a garden look much the same whatever the season.

■ **Deciduous trees and shrubs** lose all their leaves in late autumn and produce new ones in spring. Many deciduous trees and shrubs have attractive bark or interesting branch structure, or have leaves that turn colour before they fall. Ones that have showy flowers, especially those that produce edible or ornamental fruit, including berries and nuts, are useful for seasonal interest.

■ **Roses** are also deciduous shrubs, but are such a big group that they form a category on their own.

■ **Most climbers** are shrubs that can climb through another woody plant or trellis by means of suckers, twining stems or tendrils. Some shrubs with a loose habit are trained as climbing or wall shrubs by pruning and tying in to a support.

Herbaceous plants

These are plants with non-woody stems that provide flowers, and perhaps foliage interest, at some period during the year. The two main groups are hardy and half-hardy perennials, which generally die down in winter and re-emerge in spring every year (although there are a few evergreen ones), and annuals and biennials, often known as bedding plants. These are planted for bold seasonal effect and discarded at the end of their flowering period.

■ **True annuals** germinate, grow, flower, seed and die during the period of one year, but the term 'annual' is sometimes used to describe perennials (petunias, for instance) planted for temporary effect.

■ **True biennials** germinate and produce a non-flowering plant one year, then flower and die the next, but some biennials are actually perennials that have a short life or flower best in their first season (for example, wallflowers), so are treated as biennials.

■ **Bulbous plants** (those that produce shoots from underground fleshy organs known as bulbs, rhizomes, tubers or corms) are also herbaceous plants. Some popular garden plants – such as cyclamen, daffodils and snowdrops – come under this heading.

■ **Hardy plants** are those that will survive outdoors during a normal winter with minimal or no protection.

■ **Half-hardy plants**, including shrubs, annuals, perennials and bulbs, will not withstand frost and need to be over-wintered in a frost-free place, such as a well-insulated greenhouse or a cool, light room in the house.

■ **Tender plants** are those unsuitable for outdoor cultivation in the United Kingdom, and are usually grown for house or conservatory decoration.

Choosing the right plant

Always choose a plant that will not outgrow the space you have allocated for it. This may mean your garden may look rather bare for a year or two, but in the meantime you can always fill the gaps with bedding plants if you don't like the look of bare earth.

When buying from a nursery or garden centre, avoid sick or spindly plants (even if they are on sale at bargain prices) and those with weeds and moss sprouting from the top of the pot, which is a sign of poor maintenance. If lots of roots are emerging from the drainage holes at the base of the pot, it indicates that the plant should have been potted on some time ago; if the compost looks loose and fluffy, it might be that it has just been repotted, and therefore needs to re-establish before planting out.

Mail-order plants are a much better buy than they used to be, but try to find out if the company is a stock-producing nursery, or just a business buying in from elsewhere, particularly from overseas, which can be less reliable.

Before accepting offers from friends, have a look at the parent plants – if they are taking over the garden, or are pest or disease-ridden, it's best to decline politely.

Bedding plants, or annuals, will brighten up even the dullest of gardens, and are invaluable for almost instant colour, or a quick fix while you are deciding what to do with your plot on a more permanent basis.

If you have no time to raise your own bedding plants they are readily available from nurseries and garden centres at the appropriate times of year, and the range of interesting varieties is widening all the time.

Special seed mixes can be used to create an enchanting riot of colour in just one season (above). Or buy plants such as petunias, snapdragons and geraniums for instant colour in pots and borders.

Varieties of bedding plants

A bedding plant is a type of plant which is usually, though not always, raised indoors under glass either from seed or cuttings, and transplanted as a small, leafy specimen to the garden or container to produce flowers for temporary interest. There are two main types – those used for summer bedding, which are raised as half-hardy annuals and sown or raised from cuttings from late winter to mid spring for transplanting after risk of frost is past (usually mid May to early June depending on area), and those which are entirely hardy and raised from late spring to the end of June for planting in autumn to give colour the following spring.

Bedding plants are usually discarded at the end of their flowering season, although good specimens, especially of shrubby forms like fuchsias, are sometimes kept as stock

plants for cuttings. Bedding plants are usually chosen for their flowers, but others may be included for their foliage, like silver-leaved plectranthus, and a few – known as 'dot' plants – to give height to an otherwise flat bedding scheme – exotic cannas are often used for this purpose.

Container planting

Until the rise in popularity of container gardening, bedding plants were always planted out in designated beds in the open ground, but are more popular now for tubs, troughs, windowboxes and hanging baskets, or used to fill up gaps in mixed borders.

Traditionally, summer bedding plants comprise half-hardy annuals (such as *Salvia patens*), some hardy annuals like marigolds, and some half-hardy perennials treated like half-hardy annuals – petunias and geraniums, for example. A few first-year flowering hardy perennials have now been added to the list, and also many hardy plants with interesting foliage, such as trailing nepeta (*Glechoma variegata*), coleus, thyme, sage, lysimachia and bugle (ajuga).

Spring bedding plants are nearly always hardy perennials raised as biennials – sown in spring and early summer of one year to flower and be discarded afterwards the next. They include wallflowers, bellis, daisies, Brompton stocks, sweet williams, pansies and primroses.

Raising bedding plants

Most bedding plants are easily raised from seed, although summer ones require some warmth in spring for them to germinate. The alternative to this, and to buying plants ready to go out in their final positions, which can be expensive if you need a lot, is to buy plug plants. These are young plants raised in individual cells in trays, which are bought from the grower when old enough to withstand lower temperatures and are ready for potting on individually into larger plant pots or hanging baskets.

Bedding plants in the open ground should be kept well watered until established. Those in containers may need watering several times a day in hot, dry weather, and should never be allowed to dry out.

Bedding plants for different seasons and situations

Reliable summer bedding plants
- Sweet alyssum
- Fibrous and tuberous rooted begonias
- Petunias
- Tagetes (French, African and Afro-French marigolds)
- Calendula (pot marigolds)
- Lobelia
- *Salvia patens*
- Ageratum
- Impatiens (busy lizzie)
- Pelargonium (geranium)
- Ten Week stock
- Antirrhinum (snapdragon)

Foliage bedding plants
- Coleus
- *Plectranthus* 'Silver shield'
- *Lysimachia nummularia* 'Aurea' (golden creeping Jenny)
- *Senecio cineraria* (dusty miller)
- Ornamental kale (early winter)

Summer hanging basket plants
- Glechoma (trailing nepeta)
- Lotus
- Surfinia™ petunia
- Verbena
- *Pelargonium peltatum* (ivy-leaved pelargonium)
- Trailing fuchsias

'Dot' plants
- Ricinus (castor-oil plant)
- Canna
- *Grevillea robusta* (silk oak)
- Standard fuchsias
- Kochia (burning bush, summer cypress)

Spring bedding plants
- Pansy
- Viola
- Forget-me-not
- Bellis (daisy)
- Primrose and polyanthus
- Brompton stock
- Sweet william
- Wallflower

You should be able to find a herbaceous perennial for every month of the year and for every kind of situation and soil. These are also first-rate for attracting beneficial insects and wildlife into the garden, and if you are a flower arranger, you can save a fortune on bought blooms if you grow your own.

Perennials are extremely versatile, and as well as making good border plants, can also be cultivated successfully in containers, especially those varieties that have attractive leaves.

Where to get perennials

Garden centres and perennial nurseries always have a good selection for year-round interest and every kind of situation. If you want to save money and add interest to the garden, you could grow your own from seed. The seeds of most well-known and more unusual perennials are available from seed companies and are generally raised in a similar way to half-hardy annuals – sowing with some heat in spring and planting out later in the season, or the following year, when the plants are large enough.

Friends and relatives with established gardens are often glad to divide their own herbaceous perennials and pass them on.

Looking after perennials

■ Top-dress with a general fertiliser in spring. A mulch of composted bark helps to keep weeds down and the soil moist.

■ Taller varieties should be provided with stakes or metal supports as soon as growth starts in spring and tied in regularly as they increase in height. Don't wait until the plants have collapsed as you will not be able to reinstate them to look right again.

■ Cut back spent flower stems as soon as possible. This encourages new growth which may even produce a second crop of flowers, and removes untidy foliage to keep the overall appearance neat. But some

Planting perennials

1 Water the plant thoroughly and leave to drain. Remove the plant from its pot by gently supporting the stem and foliage, and tapping the container with the other hand.

2 Holding the plant by its rootball, position it in the hole at the correct depth. Pull the soil back around the plant and firm it gently into place with your foot.

3 Leave a slight depression round the base of the stem, and water into this straight after planting.

Cutting back untidy perennials

1 Once early flowering perennials like geraniums (cranesbills) have finished blooming, they become straggly and untidy. To encourage new growth, cut them back to ground level using shears.

2 Clear away the trimmings – they can go on the compost heap – then cut off neatly any remaining straggly stems.

3 Apply a sprinkling of general fertiliser and water well. The plant will soon develop a tidy mound of fresh foliage and often more flowers.

perennials, like golden rod, yarrow and Michaelmas daisies, produce seeds that are attractive to many garden birds, so leave the seeding flowerheads alone if you enjoy watching the birds feed.

■ Cut back dead stems in autumn, again leaving any seed heads which would be useful to birds.

■ Fork over between the plants lightly after cutting back, clear any weeds and top-dress with bone meal.

Use the blade of a spade to divide large, overcrowded clumps.

■ When clumps get overcrowded, split them up and replant the youngest growth round the outside of the old plant. Discard old, woody growth and roots. Replant in groups of three or five to re-establish the effect of the border in a reasonable time.

Herbaceous perennials for year-round interest

Try some of these plants – listed in order of flowering:

■ **Helleborus** (Christmas rose, Lenten rose) ■ **doronicum** (leopard's bane) ■ **hosta** (plantain lily) ■ **heuchera** (coral flower) ■ **primula** (including primroses, polyanthus, auriculas and cowslip) ■ **hardy geranium** (cranesbill) ■ **aquilegia** (columbine) ■ **lupinus** (lupin) ■ **Papaver orientale** (oriental poppy) ■ **delphinium** ■ **helenium** (sneezewort) ■ **rudbeckia** (cone flower) ■ **echinacea** (purple coneflower) ■ **sedum spectabile** (ice plant) ■ **aster** (Michaelmas daisy) ■ **schizostylis** (kaffir lily).

Strictly speaking, alpines are plants found in mountainous parts of the world, but the term has become used to describe small or miniature plants suitable for growing in a rock garden or similar situation.

An old milk crate makes a decorative holder for pots of tiny alpines.

between the cracks of a pavement, or in a sink, trough or other shallow container. It's not necessary to add rocks to have a successful alpine garden; in fact, rocks can sometimes look quite out of place.

Likes and dislikes

In general, alpines like an open, sunny position, away from the drip of trees, and good drainage. Most prefer an alkaline, gritty, not over-rich soil, although there are exceptions. When growing in containers, it's best to use a specific alpine compost; you can buy this in bags from garden centres. If planting in heavy open ground, improve the drainage and structure first by digging in horticultural sharp sand or alpine grit.

Where to grow alpines

The conventional way to grow alpines is in a rock garden, but this can be time-consuming and heavy work – large pieces of rock are needed and these must be placed so they look like a natural rocky outcrop. In addition, ordinary garden soil is unsuitable, and you need to mix in a special alpine growing medium. A rock garden should be weed free at the outset and kept that way – if weeds get a hold, you may have to dismantle the whole structure, clear out the weeds thoroughly and start again.

In a modern garden, alpines can often be grown easily and successfully on a bank, in a raised bed, as an edging to a pathway,

Choosing and buying alpines

For bank planting, look at ground-covering alpines like aubretia, arabis, campanula, alpine phlox, alyssum and gypsophila. These are reasonably quick growing and will help to cut down weeding once established. They are also ideal for edging pathways and hanging over walls, and need no maintenance apart from an annual clipping back after flowering to remove old, straggly stems and encourage new growth.

Prostrate thymes, arenaria and raoulia are useful for planting in the cracks in paving, as they are fairly tough and will withstand some walking on (although no alpines can cope with really heavy traffic).

Planting an alpine sink

1 With the plants still in their pots, arrange them into a miniaturised landscape, placing the largest plant or plants first as a focal point. Also position one or more of the biggest pieces of rock or stones.

2 Once you are satisfied with your arrangement, bed the rocks into the compost. Remove the plants from their pots and plant using a trowel. Water in well.

3 Place the remaining smaller pieces of rock or stone around the plants. Cover the compost with coarse gravel, 2-3cm deep. Tuck it carefully round the plants, without trapping their leaves.

If you are considering planting a sink garden, choose slow-growing and cushion-forming plants that will all grow at the same rate and not swamp each other, such as alpine thrift, dwarf saxifrages, houseleeks (sempervivum) and alpine pinks (dwarf dianthus). Don't overplant, as you want to be able to identify individual clumps.

Most garden centres have a reasonable selection of alpines. Pick plants that look healthy, not overgrowing the pot, and without moss or small weeds growing in the compost. Make sure that they have been watered – although alpines like free-draining conditions, they can start to die if irregularly watered before you take them home.

Planting alpines

Water pots well before planting and allow to drain. Dig holes large enough for the rootballs. Take plants out of pots, remove any crusty compost that has formed, set the plants in the holes and backfill. Cover bare soil with a layer of pea gravel or alpine grit. This looks good, lessens moisture loss through evaporation, reduces weed growth and stops foliage rotting through coming in contact with damp soil during winter.

Aftercare

Most alpines need little attention other than weeding and trimming back if they get leggy or out of shape. They do best in soils with low fertility, so feeding is unnecessary, although you can top-dress established plants in spring with a little flower fertiliser.

Tidy alpine beds and borders by cutting the straggly stems off plants that have flowered. This will stimulate the plants into producing fresh growth.

Bulbs are little power packs of colour that bring interest to the garden throughout the year. Although spring bulbs are the ones most widely planted, those that flower in summer and autumn are also worth growing for extra effect in the border or container.

Buying bulbs

Bulbs can be bought at the garden centre, and also by mail order from companies specialising in bulbs and similar items. Bulbs bought by mail order are often your best bet, because not only have they been graded for size and performance to give you what you are looking for, but they have been stored in ideal conditions in terms of temperature and moisture. If you prefer to choose your own bulbs from a garden centre or shop, be wary of bulbs kept in warm conditions, as they are more likely to be soft and actively growing than those kept in a cool, dry atmosphere.

The best flowers come from the biggest bulbs, so choose the largest you can afford. The 'second-size' bulbs are more economical for naturalising in large quantities. With loose and pre-packed bulbs, look for clean, firm and plump examples, with no obvious root or shoot growth. Avoid those that are dirty, soft, damaged, shrivelled, or showing signs of mould or pale, forced shoots and roots. Try to plant bulbs as soon as possible after buying or delivery.

Planting bulbs

■ Spring flowering bulbs, except tulips, are planted from the end of August to the end of November for the best results.

Easy bulbs for every season

Spring: Large-flowered crocus, daffodils and narcissi, scillas, chionodoxa, hyacinths, tulips, bluebells.
Summer: Alliums, ixias, sparaxis, gladioli.
Autumn: Gladioli, colchicums.
Winter: Snowdrops, species crocus.

Naturalising bulbs in grass

1 Cut the outline of a large 'H' through the turf using a spade. This makes it easier to peel back the turf from the middle to expose a rectangle of soil. Loosen the soil underneath with a fork.
2 Fork in bone meal at a rate of 15g per square metre. Then scatter the bulbs over the exposed soil and press each one in gently; they should be at least 2-3cm apart.
3 Make sure the bulbs are upright before carefully replacing the turf.
4 Firm the turf gently with your hand and, if necessary, fill the joints with fine soil.

Planting bulbs in the border

1 Dig out a large planting hole wide enough for the bulbs to be at least their own width apart and deep enough so they are covered with soil to two or three times their height.

2 Scatter a little bone meal over the base of the hole and lightly fork in, then water gently before positioning the bulbs.

3 Gently cover bulbs with soil, tamp the surface firm with the back of a rake and label the area.

Tulip bulbs should be planted in November. Summer-flowering bulbs are planted in late spring and early summer, when the ground has warmed up and the danger of frost has passed.

Deadheading

Deadhead bulbs by pinching off the flowerheads, but leave the stalks and leaves intact to die down naturally.

■ Bulbs in borders look better flowering in informal groups. Before planting, add plenty of garden compost or well-rotted manure and dig some coarse sand or grit into a heavy soil to improve drainage.

■ Smaller bulbs, such as snowdrops or crocuses, add charming informality to areas of a lawn or wild garden.

■ Before planting in grass, mow the area as short as possible. After flowering you must wait at least six weeks before mowing the grass, to allow the bulb foliage to die down naturally and ensure flowers in future years.

Lifting and storing corms in winter

In areas where the weather is mild, gladioli, ixias (corn lilies) and sparaxis (harlequin flowers) corms may be left in the ground throughout the year. Elsewhere, when the leaves begin to brown in October, the corms should be lifted, cleaned and dried off, then stored in a cool, dry, frost-free place until the following year.

Ask gardeners for their favourite flower and the rose would probably come out top. There is a rose for almost every situation, from tiny patio varieties and classic bush roses to romantic climbers and ramblers to festoon a fence or archway, and low-growing species for effective ground cover.

Site and soil

Roses need sun for at least three-quarters of the day. Avoid shady and exposed windy sites. Neutral or slightly acid, medium soil, with a pH of 6.5, is best. Improve heavy and light soils by adding as much compost or manure as possible. Apply a specific rose fertiliser twice a year by scattering a handful round each plant in spring and again soon after midsummer, when the first flush of bloom is over. Mulch with well-rotted compost, farmyard manure or bark after feeding in spring, and top up if necessary after the summer feed.

Planting roses

Before planting, cut out any damaged or diseased shoots from the top growth and trim back tough roots by a third. Make the planting hole wide enough for the roots to spread out and deep enough for the budding union to be 2.5cm below the soil surface. Work a small handful of rose fertiliser into

Be firm with your boot when filling in the soil around a new rose.

the soil at the bottom of the hole, then set the plant in the hole. Work in soil round the roots so that there are no air pockets, then fill in the hole and tread soil down firmly.

Wooden posts give excellent support to climbing roses.

Training climbing roses

■ When growing a rose on a wall, tie the shoots to wires threaded through vine eyes driven into the brickwork and stretched horizontally about 45cm apart up the wall.
■ When training a rose up a pillar, spiral it round the support.

Rose hedges

Many shrub roses make excellent hedges. Train spreading shrub roses along horizontal wires strung between posts or on a chain-link fence. Upright shrub roses rarely need such training.

■ **Arthur Bell** (cluster flowered/floribunda) Large, golden-yellow flowers, fragrant with glossy, leathery leaves.
■ **Peer Gynt** (LF/HT) Yellow, shaded orange. Compact, bushy habit.
■ **Just Joey** (LF/HT) Coppery-orange, veined red, pales to apricot towards edge of petals.
■ **Hannah Gordon** (CF/F1) White, shading to cherry-pink. Deep bronze-green foliage.

Miniature and patio roses
■ **Orange Sunblaze** Orange-red.
■ **Gentle Touch** Pink, tall miniature.
■ **Top Marks** Orange vermilion patio rose. Abundance of blooms.
■ **Sweet Dream** Orange-yellow to apricot.
■ **City Lights** Deep yellow, very fragrant.

Climbing roses
■ **Danse du Feu** Orange-red, medium grower. Tolerates shade; can be grown on north wall.
■ **Golden Showers** Golden-yellow, upright, branching habit, medium height. Good for training up pillars.

Secateurs and a pair of gloves are all you need for deadheading.

Deadheading
The regular removal of spent blooms (deadheading) encourages a repeat-flowering rose to produce a second flush later in the season. Don't deadhead species roses or any other roses grown for their decorative hips.

Recommended roses

Bush roses
■ **Royal William** (large flowered/hybrid tea) Crimson, fragrant, strong growing; tallish.

■ **Silver Jubilee** (LF/HT) Salmon-pink, shaded peach (above). Fresh fragrance, disease resistant.

■ **Compassion** Salmon-pink, HT-shaped flowers all summer, very fragrant (above). Strong, healthy growth.
■ **Antique** Rose-pink with pale pink centres, cabbage rose-shaped blooms. Vigorous, disease resistant.

■ **Madame Alfred Carrière** White flowers from pale pink buds. Fragrant. Easily trained. Tolerates a north-facing position.

Rambler roses

■ **Alberic Barbier** Yellow buds opening creamy-white, double and fragrant. Almost evergreen foliage.

■ **Albertine** Copper, fading to salmon-pink, scented, profuse.

■ **New Dawn** Shell-pink, fragrant, repeat flowering. Strong, healthy growth.

Shrub roses

■ **Rosa xanthina 'Canarybird'** Very early, single, yellow, fragrant flowers. Tall, arching.

■ **Hybrid musk 'Buff Beauty'** Masses of apricot-yellow flowers, heavily scented. Long flowering season. Medium height.

■ **'Ballerina'** Bushy, huge heads of small, single, pale pink flowers with white eye.

■ **'Nevada'** Semi-double, fragrant, white flowers in May and June, second flush in August to summer's end, Sturdy habit up to 2m.

■ **Rosa moyesii 'Geranium'** Red flowers followed by bottle-shaped hips. Compact.

■ **'Graham Thomas'** New English rose with yellow, fragrant flowers all the season (above). Strong growth, medium-tall habit.

Ground-cover roses

■ **Essex** Pink, repeat flowering. Bushy.

■ **Partridge** Wide spreading, white, single or semi-double flowers.

■ **Red Blanket** Rose-red, semi-double heads, perpetual flowering. Fairly prostrate.

■ **Flower Carpet Series** Pink, coral, red, yellow and white on low-spreading bushes.

Pruning climbing roses

1 Prune out all dead stems and ends of stems, cutting back to healthy wood, then cut out two or three of the oldest branches, either to ground level or to where a strong replacement stem originates.

2 Stimulate flowering by shortening all sideshoots to leave two to four buds.

3 Tie new stems to their supports to make an even spread of branches; some may need retying to avoid overcrowding or crossing growth.

Basic moderate pruning of shrub roses

1 Cut out all dead stems and trim parts that are damaged or diseased back to healthy wood, which will show a white cut surface.

2 Remove thin, spindly shoots, and any that cross one another or that are growing into the centre of the plant. Also cut out or pull off any suckers.

3 Shorten the remaining strong, healthy branches by half to an outward-facing bud or shoot. Compost or dispose of the prunings.

4 Prune out one or two of the oldest branches to ground level using long-handled pruners, to stimulate strong new growth.

Rose pruning made easy

With warmer winters becoming more frequent, in most parts of the UK roses can be pruned any time from November to March. In colder areas of the country, though, it's best to leave the job until early spring. In this case, long shoots should be shortened in autumn to prevent wind damage and root-rock.

For all bush roses, including hybrid teas, floribundas, patio roses, standards and shrub roses, cut out all dead, diseased and crossing shoots and open up the centre of the bush. Cut back growth made in the current year by a third to a half, to an outward-pointing bud. Shrub roses only need this treatment every two or three years.

■ **Miniature roses** Trim lightly with shears or secateurs.

■ **Ground-cover roses** If they become straggly or out of control, cut back with shears. Remove upward-growing stems and thin overcrowded growth with secateurs.

■ **Climbing roses** With secateurs, remove dead, dying, diseased, straggly and badly placed shoots and tie new growths horizontally to the supports, or wind the long shoots of pillar-trained roses round the post or obelisk. Some seasons, cut out one or two really old branches with a pruning saw or heavy-duty loppers to encourage new growth from near the base.

■ **Rambler roses** Cut out with secateurs all the shoots that have flowered, immediately after flowering. Tie in new shoots – these will flower the following summer. If there is a new shoot lower down on an existing shoot that has already flowered, prune back to this.

Shrubs

Shrubs are the backbone of the garden, providing foliage and flower colour in summer and structure in winter, while evergreens keep the interest alive throughout the year. No garden is too small for at least one or two, and practically every shrub can be grown in a container, for a few years at least.

The right shrubs can make all the difference in a garden; standards along a fence add a formal structure to these flowerbeds.

Shrubs may be grown in a bed or border on their own, but in most modern gardens they are best combined with other types of plants in a mixed planting. Many can be planted in a lawn or gravel, or suitable varieties can be planted slightly closer than normal along a boundary to make an interesting informal hedge.

Flowering shrubs give a boost to the garden when in bloom, but can look rather dull when not in flower, so where space is limited, choose ones that have additional qualities, such as variegated foliage, and combine them with interesting evergreens or those with coloured bark.

Find out before you buy how tall and wide-spreading a shrub will get after, say, five or ten years. If a flowering shrub is likely to outgrow its space, look for a more suitable variety. It's not a good idea to cut it back to make it smaller, as you will cut off all the potential flowering shoots. A shrub grown for its foliage, though, can be kept smaller by regular pruning.

Shrubs need a top dressing of a balanced fertiliser every year in spring. Those growing in the ground benefit from a bark mulch every year after feeding, which helps to keep the soil moist.

Shrubs and wildlife

Try to include a few shrubs to attract wildlife into the garden. These include: buddleja, sambucus (ornamental elder), cotoneaster, ilex (holly), ribes (flowering currant) and *Viburnum opulus* (guelder rose). All shrubs, even when quite small, make possible nesting habitat for birds in summer and roosting sites in winter.

Shrubs for modern gardens

■ **Aucuba japonica 'Variegata' (spotted laurel)** A variegated evergreen that will survive almost anywhere. Female plants produce berries if planted with a male.

■ **Berberis darwinii** Medium-sized evergreen with small, bright green, spiny leaves and red-tinted new shoots. Golden-yellow flowers in late spring and early summer, followed by blue-black berries.

■ **Buddleja davidii (butterfly bush)** Attracts butterflies when in flower. Flower spikes can be white, blue, lavender or purple. Cut back hard in spring.

■ **Choisya ternata 'Sundance' (golden Mexican orange blossom)** Small evergreen shrub with nutmeg-scented leaves and masses of fragrant, white flowers in late spring and early summer.

■ **Cornus alba (red-stemmed dogwood)** A shrub grown for its brightly coloured bark and brilliant autumn colour. White flowers in late spring, then white berries, turning blue, then black. Cut back hard every two years for best bark colour.

■ **Cotinus coggygria 'Royal Purple'** Deciduous shrub with rich purple leaves and purplish bark in winter. Fluffy flowers give a 'smoke' effect.

■ **Forsythia** Spring-flowering shrub. Various sizes and variegated forms obtainable.

■ **Hypericum (St John's wort)** Small or medium-sized semi-evergreen shrub with showy, yellow flowers (see below).

Clusters of ribes flowers bloom early and attract bees.

■ **Philadelphus coronarius 'Variegatus'** Medium-sized, variegated mock orange, with perfumed, creamy-white flowers in June.

■ **Ribes sanguineum (flowering currant)** A small to medium-sized shrub, flowering early in spring, attracts early bees and other insects. Flowers deep red to white.

■ **Spiraea arguta (bridal wreath)** White flowers wreath the branches in spring/early summer.

■ **Syringa (lilac)** Can be pruned hard after flowering without affecting flowers later on.

■ **Viburnum tinus** Medium to large evergreen shrub with blush white flowerheads in late winter and spring.

■ **Weigela florida 'Variegata'** A small shrub as attractive in leaf as in flower, with pale yellow and green foliage sometimes tinged pink; tubular, pink flowers in June.

Pruning shrubs

If you buy well-shaped shrubs you shouldn't need to prune them for the first three to five years. Pruning to remove dead, damaged or diseased wood can generally be done at any time of year.

Shrubs flowering before midsummer

Plants that produce flowers on the previous year's growth, such as forsythia and philadelphus, bloom mainly in spring and

A splash of colour is provided by yellow *Hypericum cerastioides*.

The one-third prune

1 As soon as the flowers fade, it's time to prune away a third of a leafy overgrown shrub.

2 Cut out any weak, spindly shoots and stems that cross or crowd each other out. Use a sharp pair of secateurs.

3 Remove a proportion of the oldest branches just above ground level or to a low, strong sideshoot. You may need to use a pruning saw for this.

4 Remove a third of the growth annually, so that no branch on the shrub is more than three years old. This will admit light to the shrub and maintain a good shape.

early summer. Prune as soon as the flowers fade. Cut out a quarter to a third of older flowering shoots, cutting back to the highest new shoot or bud. The plant will then make new growth in summer that will produce flowers the following spring.

Shrubs flowering after midsummer

Plants that produce flowers on the current year's growth, such as *Buddleja davidii*, large-leaved hebes and lavatera, usually bloom from midsummer into autumn.

Prune in early spring, just before new growth. Cut back last season's flowering stems and any weak shoots. The harder you prune, the more new growth will be made. Flowers will develop on this new growth.

Young foliage or coloured stems

These plants, such as *Cornus alba, Salix alba* and *Sambucus nigra* are pruned in early spring to encourage abundant new growth for summer and brighter stems for winter. Prune back all of the previous year's growth to near ground level or back to an established framework of branches. To avoid weakening the shrub over time, hard pruning is best done no more often than every two or three years.

Evergreen foliage

Evergreen shrubs, such as *Lonicera nitida* and *Prunus lusitanica*, are pruned to keep them in shape. The best times to prune are late spring and summer, but check to make

Pruning an overgrown deciduous shrub

1 Take a close look at your overgrown shrub in winter: even with evergreens it's easier to see the structure then, especially at the end of winter when frost injuries should be apparent.

2 First cut out all dead, damaged and diseased wood, then remove any weak, spindly stems.

3 Using loppers or a pruning saw, cut out any stems that interfere with the growth of a more important branch, or that cross the centre of the shrub. Then thin out any overcrowded stems.

4 Only then prune the main flowering or structural branches, according to variety.

5 In many cases you need to cut back almost to the base of shoots that have recently flowered to restrict size, but prune less severely if you want a large shrub.

6 Pruning admits more light and air to the centre of the plant, promoting healthy growth.

sure birds are not nesting in them first. Avoid pruning in frosty weather because this can cause damage to the cut shoots. Cut out any unwanted growth to maintain shape and size. Shorten excessively long shoots and thin overcrowded bushes.

Rejuvenating an old shrub

Don't worry if you have any untidy, overgrown shrubs as they can easily be given a new lease of life. In the first year, in early spring, cut out up to a third of the old wood as low down in the plant as possible. This action will encourage plenty of strong new shoots. When the new growth is at its maximum – probably midsummer – trim it back by a third. In the second year, cut back the remaining old wood to leave only the new growth from the previous season.

True climbers are plants that are capable of supporting themselves on a structure by means of tendrils, suckers, or twining leaves or stems. In addition, you will often find listed as climbers, plants with a spreading or weak-stemmed habit that can easily be tied in and pruned to cover a support.

Three varieties of purple clematis intertwine on a summer bower.

Pruning clematis

It's not essential to prune clematis, but most gardeners do some cutting back. Large flowered hybrids flowering before the end of June, such as 'The President' and 'Nelly Moser', are pruned after flowering by thinning out the shoots. Overgrown plants can be cut hard back, but may not flower as freely next season. Large-flowered hybrids flowering from July onwards, such as 'Gypsy Queen' and 'Comtesse de Bouchard', are cut back to within 15cm of the ground in spring. Species clematis (such as *C. Montana*) are tidied after flowering.

Climbers are useful for adding a 3-D effect. In a tight space, they give the opportunity to grow a plant in limited space, especially with roses. They can be used to cover a trellis, pergola, arch, wall or fence. Twining and tendril-producing forms are most suitable for an open-work structure, while lax, or wall, shrubs are better for training on a trellis, wall or fence using wires. Climbers that cling to their supports with suckers, such as ivy and Virginia creeper, are best on a wall, but tend to leave suckers behind when they are pulled off; these are difficult to remove, so think carefully before planting. They don't damage surfaces or kill trees, but may smother young tree growths.

Always choose the right climber for the aspect on which it is to grow. Many clematis, for example, will burn up in the hot sun of a south or west-facing wall, but will thrive and produce brighter-coloured flowers in shade, while a hot wall is just the place for a sun lover like actinidia or jasmine.

Recommended climbers

■ **Actinidia kolomikta** Grown mainly for its green, pink and white leaves, but mature plants have white, fragrant flowers in June.
■ **Ceanothus dentatus** Evergreen shrub often trained against a wall.
■ **Clematis** Huge family with great variety and spread, and flowers almost all year round according to variety.
■ **Cotoneaster horizontalis** Self-supporting if placed close to a wall. Lots of pink buds, opening white, followed by red berries.
■ **Hedera (ivy)** Many varieties with small, medium and large, often variegated leaves.

The yellow blossoms of *Jasminium nudiflorum* brighten up the winter garden.

Planting a climber

1 Dig a hole larger and deeper than is needed for the climber's rootball and tip a bonemeal and compost mixture into the bottom of the hole. Turn the climber gently out of its pot.

2 If the roots are congested, tease them out, then place the rootball in the hole and plant fractionally deeper than the original level of compost in the container. Back-fill the hole with soil, firming it down gently with your foot.

3 Water thoroughly. If the stems are long enough, tie them to a support. If not, place canes at an angle to encourage young stems to grow towards the fence or wall support.

■ **Hydrangea petiolaris (climbing hydrangea)** A self-clinging climber with flat plates of white flowers in early summer.
■ **Jasminum (jasmine)** *Jasminium nudiflorum* is a winter-flowering shrub. Others flower in summer; many are scented.
■ **Lonicera (honeysuckle)** A twining climber with attractive, mostly fragrant flowers.
■ **Parthenocissus tricuspidata (Virginia creeper)** Self clinging, planted for its showy green leaves and spectacular autumn colour.
■ **Pyracantha (firethorn)** Easy to train as a wall plant. White flowers in early summer followed by red, orange or yellow berries.
■ **Wisteria** Late spring/early summer climber with long racemes of white, pink, purple or blue flowers.

Pruning

Many climbers require little or no regular pruning. Self-clinging types, such as Virginia creeper, ivy and climbing hydrangea, need nothing other than the removal of unwanted growth, like that growing across a window or into the roof. Clipping over in late summer keeps the plants tidy.

Shrubs that have been trained against a wall, for example pyracantha and ceanothus, should be pruned after flowering, cutting back to shape, but those bearing berries later in the year should only have young growth that has not borne flowers removed.

Twining forms, like honeysuckle, don't need pruning at all. But to keep the plants in check and encourage young growth they can be shortened back from late autumn to early spring.

Pruning and training climbers

1 Space out main stems evenly and at an angle from the vertical. Secure them to their support using soft twine tied in a figure of eight.

2 Trim back wayward stems to just above a leaf joint. You may need to do this regularly for vigorous climbers.

There is a tree for nearly every garden. Even where space is tight, you can plant a small or slow-growing tree in a large tub to restrict growth enough to make it manageable. But choose the tree to suit your site – nothing looks sadder than a large one chopped back because it has outgrown its space.

In spring and early summer ornamental trees come into their own, with flowers of every colour and size. If you only have room for one or two, trees with attractive fruit extend the season of interest, and those with leaves that change colour during spring and autumn also liven up a compact plot.

Remember that the trees you buy from the nursery or garden centre are only young, and will have an impact on the light and moisture in your garden as they grow. Find out the height and spread of your chosen tree in five, ten and 20 years before you buy so you don't have to remove it later because it has made the area too shady or too dry, obscured a favourite view, or smothered other plants.

Use a yellow-leaved shrub such as *Gleditsia triacanthos* 'Sunburst' for a splash of sunshine among more sombre plants.

Never plant forest trees (native forms of oak, ash, cherry or beech) in a domestic garden as they will eventually grow too large and their roots may damage buildings or drains.

A newly planted tree usually needs support to prevent wind rock. Secure the trunk to a stout stake with tree ties that will expand as the tree grows. Or use two stakes set a little way apart with a horizontal piece of wood between them near the top, to which the tree is tied, or a stake driven well into the ground at an angle – the young tree is secured firmly to this where the trunk and the stake meet. Make sure that the tree does not rub against the stake or it may suffer serious, permanent damage.

Trees for modern gardens

■ **Acer x pseudoplatanus 'Brilliantissimum'** A small to medium-sized sycamore with leaves opening shrimp pink, turning yellow and finally green in summer.

■ **Acer negundo 'Harlequin'** A pretty tree kept small by annual cutting back. Green and white leaves with pink young growths.

■ **Betula utilis 'Silver Shadow'** A lovely birch with brilliant white young wood and bark, suitable for a modest garden.

■ **Catalpa bignonioides 'Aurea'** Yellow-leaved form of the Indian bean tree, with large, velvety leaves. Mature trees bear hanging, white, foxglove-like flowers.

■ **Gleditsia triacanthos 'Sunburst'** Golden yellow, small to medium with ferny foliage (choose 'Ruby Lace' for a small garden).

■ **Magnolia stellata** A small to medium-sized magnolia with pure white flowers opening like big stars in spring.

■ **Malus 'Rudolph'** Leaves open bronze-red, and turn green, with bright, rosy red flowers and orange-yellow fruit.

The brilliant foliage of an acer can be used to lift a gloomy corner.

■ **Prunus 'Pink Perfection'** Medium sized with double pink blossom in spring.
■ **Salix purpurea 'Pendula'** A weeping willow for modern gardens with thin, pendulous branches, long, narrow grey-blue leaves, purple bark and slender catkins all along the branches.

■ **Sorbus aucuparia 'Sheerwater seedling'** Upright mountain ash (rowan); heads of white flowers in spring followed by orange-red berries and fiery autumn foliage.

Pruning trees

No regular pruning of established trees is required, but branches crossing each other and diseased, dead and dying wood should be removed as soon as you spot them. As young trees grow, you may need to remove the bottom branches to open up the ground underneath.

If you have to prune a tree, it's always better to remove a whole limb than 'snip-prune' the ends of the branches. Cut back to 1-2cm of the trunk or main branch; this encourages the wound to heal and callous over. In most instances, you don't need to paint the cut with a sealing compound – the exception being members of the cherry family (ornamental cherries, plums, peaches and almonds), which are prone to infection through large cuts if not sealed.

Pruning a young tree

1 The autumn after planting, cut out the sideshoots (or feathers) on the lowest third of the stem to clean the trunk. This is sometimes known as 'feathering'.

2 Shorten sideshoots on the next third of the trunk by half, and leave the top third unpruned. Repeat this each year until the clean trunk is the required height, above which natural branching can be allowed to develop.

Raising the crown

1 When the tree is dormant, work your way up the trunk, removing enough of the lowest branches to raise the tree's crown, or head, of branches.

2 While the tree retains its distinct profile, the crown is then carried on a taller trunk.

Every garden has a place for a conifer. There are examples ranging in height and spread from many metres tall and suitable only for the largest areas, to just a few centimetres, making them ideal for rock gardens or containers.

Conifers come in foliage colours from green and blue to gold and pale cream, and many different shapes to add form to every design. They don't look the same year-round, as new spring shoots can be quite different in colour, and many varieties turn red or bronze in winter. Most are evergreen, but *Ginkgo biloba*, the maidenhair tree, and larix (larch) lose their leaves after turning bright yellow in autumn.

Most conifers prefer well-drained but moist soil. If your garden is dry, you will find that junipers will cope better than most. Conifers associate well with heathers and, in the case of dwarf forms, alpines and rock garden plants. You can plant them together to form a bed entirely of conifers or add them to a mixed or shrub border.

When buying conifers, do your research first, as the size of a tree in the nursery is no indication of its final height and spread. A small tree may grow to be a giant, while large specimens of dwarf varieties can be planted to create instant effect.

Coping with overgrown leylandii

A Leyland cypress hedge can reach 9m or more, which makes Leyland hedges time-consuming and awkward to trim. For a drastic remedy, you can cut them down to a metre or two, providing they have some green growth below this, and hope that they recover. To be safe, do this in several stages and get professional help if the hedge is taller than 3m.

For a quick way to cover up any dead, lower branches that have turned brown, plant periwinkle (vinca) at the base of the hedge.

Easy conifers for modern gardens

■ **Abies balsamea 'Hudsonia'** A dwarf form of the Balsam fir, with aromatic foliage and a compact, rounded shape.

■ **Chamaecyparis lawsoniana 'Summer Snow'** A small to medium conifer with feathery foliage and white new shoots, turning cream then pale green. A good specimen conifer for a lawn or in gravel.

Planting a container-grown conifer

1 Fork plenty of compost or similar well-rotted organic material into the soil, then dig a hole two to three times the width of the plant's rootball.

2 Stand the plant in the hole, keeping the rootball intact, and adjust the planting depth so that the old soil mark on the stem is at surface level.

3 After back-filling the hole with soil, gently shake the tree once or twice to settle the soil around its roots. Then level the soil surface, water and cover the area with a thick organic mulch. Continue to water well in dry weather, so that the new tree does not dry out.

Trimming a formal conifer hedge

1 Allow conifers to grow about 60cm above the desired height before cutting. Run a string between two canes at the cutting height, which should be around 15cm below the ultimate level. This will encourage new bushy growth at the top.

2 Trim the sides, starting at the bottom and working upwards, and making the hedge narrower at the top than it is at the base. Wear goggles and gloves when using a powered hedge-trimmer and, if electric, always use a circuit breaker (RCD) for safety.

3 Cut the top of the hedge along your guideline, tapering the edges rather than leaving a flat, wide top. Do not overreach; if necessary, set up a ladder or trestles and make sure they stand on a firm, level base. Get a helper to steady the bottom of a ladder while you are working.

■ **Cryptomeria japonica 'Elegans'**
A medium to large conifer with feathery foliage turning bronze-red in winter. A good specimen for a large shrubbery or lawn.

■ **Juniperus sabina 'Tamariscifolia'** This produces tiers of horizontal, grey-green branches. Often used for bank planting.

■ **Juniperus communis 'Compressa'**
A compact, slow-growing, upright conifer; makes a good specimen in a rock garden.

■ **Picea abies 'Pygmaea'** A tiny, slow-growing form of Christmas tree, suitable for a small rockery or sink garden.

■ **Pinus mugo 'Mops'** A miniature form of mountain pine with a dense, bushy form and comparatively long needles. It's extremely lime tolerant, so will thrive in chalky soils.

■ **Taxus baccata 'Standishii'** A slow-growing, golden yew with an upright habit.

It's useful for 'dot' planting, but can be used as a slow-growing, easy-maintenance hedge.

■ **Thuja plicata 'Smaragd'** A form of western red cedar with a conical habit, fresh green foliage and restrained growth, making it an ideal candidate for a hedge and a much better choice than the rampant Leyland or Lawson's cypresses.

Pruning conifers

Conifers are best pruned or trimmed in late summer, at the end of the nesting season. They should not be cut back further than the green growth, as, with the exception of yew, they are unlikely to shoot again. Conifer hedges, especially fast-growing ones like leylandii should be cut every year to prevent their getting out of hand. Start trimming a conifer hedge well before it has reached its required height and width.

Although you may not be able to grow enough vegetables to feed your household throughout the year, there is great satisfaction in raising even one or two crops. Start with ones that are easy to grow, then as you gain experience progress to those requiring a bit more skill.

Rows of colourful salad leaves and strappy onions make a striking, edible bed. Herb beds surround the statue of Pan.

Where to grow

Vegetables need an open, sunny site and good, fertile soil. You might find it easier to start with a small area, and increase it later if you need to. If your garden is too small or too shady for a vegetable plot, try growing a few plants of your favourite kinds in raised beds on the patio. For best results, these need to be 30cm deep and filled with John Innes No. 3 Compost. The best size for each bed is 1m x 1m, which allows you to grow a reasonable quantity of your chosen crops and access them easily from all sides. Alternatively, grow vegetables in large tubs of multipurpose compost. You can even grow some types – ideally the ones with attractive foliage, like carrots, beetroot or red-leaved lettuces – at the front of borders.

How to grow

Most easy, popular vegetables are grown from seed in spring, when the soil and the air temperature have started to warm up. About two weeks before you intend to sow, give a dressing of a balanced fertiliser according to the manufacturer's instructions. Before sowing, rake the soil to make a fine seedbed, or level the compost in your containers or raised beds.

When you are ready to sow, make shallow drills in the seedbed with the back of a rake or a draw hoe (or the edge of a trowel if you are growing in raised beds). To get the line straight, use a garden line or, in raised beds, a cane laid across the bed. Water along the drill so the seeds start off in damp soil.

Sow salad seeds thinly in shallow moist drills set in crumbly soil.

The instructions on the packet will tell you how deep to sow, but, as a general rule, sow seeds no deeper than their own diameter – so small seeds are sown just 1mm deep and larger ones 2-5mm deep. Sow the seed as thinly as possible, lightly cover with soil (or compost in a raised bed) and use the back of a rake to tamp the surface level.

TIP

Potatoes may be easy to grow, but they take up a lot of space – and are cheap to buy anyway. Try growing vegetables that will taste their best picked fresh, or those that would be expensive if bought in the supermarket or greengrocer.

The seedlings will emerge between one and three weeks after sowing, according to type. When they are large enough to handle, thin out to the recommended distances suggested on the seed packets. Keep the young plants watered well after they appear, especially after thinning out. You may need to thin two or three times at intervals in order for the vegetables to develop properly. Don't throw away your 'thinnings' – the baby leaves of beetroot, carrots, spinach, radishes and lettuce make a delicious mixed-leaf salad.

It's better to sow many quick-maturing crops, such as finger carrots, lettuce, spring onions, radishes, spinach and turnips, little and often, to avoid having a glut early in the season and nothing later on.

Some vegetables, like cabbage, broccoli, cauliflower, runner beans and leeks, can be bought as young plants from the garden centre, which saves you having to sow and transplant them yourself.

Onions and cabbages thrive in the well-tended vegetable plot.

Easy vegetables for the first-time gardener

Salad leaves: lettuce, mixed salad leaves (rocket, lamb's lettuce, land cress and so forth, which seed companies sell in packets as mixtures); radishes; spring onions.
Root vegetables: turnips, carrots, beetroot.
Onions and shallots: from sets sold in garden centres; leeks (from baby plants).
Leaf vegetables: spinach beet, Swiss chard (easily grown from seed).
Brassicas (cabbage family): cabbage, sprouting broccoli (from bought-in plants).
Peas, broad beans, runner beans: from bought-in plants.

The flavour of bought fruit, however fresh, bears no resemblance to that of fruit picked from your garden and eaten straightaway. You may not have room for an orchard, but every garden has enough space for a small fruit crop of some sort, and most kinds are so easy to grow.

Types of fruit

Soft fruit

This kind of fruit includes strawberries, fruit borne on bushes, including gooseberries, blackcurrants, red and white currants, and cane fruits such as raspberries, blackberries and loganberries. These can be grown in the open ground in your garden, but strawberries and bush fruits can also be planted in containers – strawberries in pots, troughs, window boxes and growing bags, and bush fruits in large tubs such as half barrels. Raspberries can be tied into wires or trellises as screens, and blackberries, loganberries and other blackberry hybrids can be trained as climbers on walls.

Planting and pruning Plant container-grown soft fruit in John Innes No. 3 Compost, and top-dress with a slow-release, balanced feed every spring. Trim strawberry plants back at the end of the fruiting season, and cut out fruited canes (stems) of raspberries and blackberries. Prune blackcurrants by removing a third of the old branches every year after fruiting, and gooseberries and red and white currants by thinning out overcrowded branches and shortening back the sideshoots.

Tree fruit – or top fruit

This includes fruits normally grown on trees or large bushes, like apples, pears, plums, cherries, peaches and nectarines. The fruit varieties are grafted onto rootstocks that regulate the growth of the tree or bush; for most garden situations a dwarfing or semi-dwarfing rootstock is the most suitable. You can also grow small fruit trees in large containers, in which case choose a dwarfing rootstock – although growing in a container will also eventually slow down growth. The labels on most top-fruit bushes will tell you

Cut fruited raspberry canes right to the ground in autumn.

A dwarf apple tree grows well in a large container.

what kinds of rootstock they have. Otherwise ask a member of staff at the nursery or garden centre for recommendations.

Where space is limited, trained fruit trees – cordons, fans and espaliers – are a better choice than trees or bushes. These can be supported by trellis or post and wire framework, or planted against sunny fences or walls. They are more expensive than bushes because of the extra work that has gone into their training. The nursery will advise on further training and pruning.

Some fruit trees are self-fertile – they can set a crop without a pollinator – but many varieties require another tree of the same kind but a different variety to produce a crop. Again, your nursery can advise you.

Pruning fruit trees Good-quality fruit trees and bushes will come already pruned, with a well-shaped head and a framework of branches that will last the life of the tree. Heavy pruning is not necessary – it encourages the growth of long, often badly placed shoots and can delay fruiting. All you need to do is remove dead, dying, diseased and weak material, crossing branches and those growing into the centre. There is no need to paint large cuts with a sealing paint in the case of apples and pears, but you should seal cuts on plums, cherries, peaches and nectarines immediately with a proprietary pruning compound to prevent fungal infections entering the wounds.

Prune apples and pears while dormant (from late autumn to early spring), and plums, cherries and other members of the cherry family in warmer weather, as many diseases that can affect them thrive at low temperatures.

Easy fruit for beginners

Soft fruits

■ strawberry: 'Elsanta', 'Pegasus'
■ raspberry: 'Glen Moy', 'Malling Admiral'
■ blackberry: 'Silvan' ■ blackcurrant: 'Ben Connan', 'Ben Sarek' ■ redcurrant: 'Junifer', 'Rovada'.

Tree fruits

■ apple: 'James Grieve', 'Fiesta' ■ pear: 'Concorde', 'Conference' ■ plum: 'Victoria', 'Early Transparent Gage' ■ cherry: 'Stella', 'Summer Sun' ■ peach: 'Peregrine', 'Rochester' ■ nectarine: 'Lord Napier'.

An old chimney pot makes a fine planter for strawberries.

Prolific redcurrants are easy to grow and make great jelly.

Planting in containers

Containers come in myriad designs and materials and offer tremendous scope for planting. They don't need to cost a fortune, and even discarded household items, such as old buckets and large pans, can be put to good use as temporary planters.

There are containers for every situation, and in a vast range of materials, from terracotta and lead to lightweight plastic and wood.

Choosing your containers

There is a choice of pots, planters, troughs, barrels and urns to suit all budgets, as well as hanging baskets and windowboxes. To achieve a sense of harmony, it is best to limit the choice of materials and rely on a variety of shapes and sizes to create interest. Choose shapes, materials and colours that harmonise with your house and garden.

Terracotta containers

Terracotta pots are a traditional choice; they look good almost anywhere and suit most plants. Make sure they are made of frost-proof material if you want to use them year-round. Terracotta is porous, so the compost in it dries out quickly, unless the sides of the pot are lined with polythene. It breaks easily, so position pots out of harm's way.

Other containers

Wood is natural and long lasting, and looks good in almost any setting. Styles vary from smart Versailles tubs, often placed in pairs, to rustic half-barrels. Check that the metal bands of a barrel are sound and secure; you may need to drill drainage holes in the base. **Galvanised metal containers** usually come in simple shapes such as troughs and florists' buckets, and best suit minimal garden styles. The thin metal leaves roots vulnerable to fluctuations in temperature: line containers with a thick layer of newspaper to prevent roots getting too hot in summer, and don't use outdoors in winter. **Glazed pots** bring colour into the garden, but the designs and shades do not suit all gardens and bright colours can date quickly. As with terracotta, not all pots are frost-proof, but the glazing does prevent water loss through the sides.

Natural and reconstituted stone containers are costly. Classic designs, such as urns, are best suited to grand or fairly formal gardens; simple stone troughs look good anywhere. Use an urn as a focal point in the garden, rather than grouping it with other pots on a patio. They are heavy and difficult to move. **Containers in man-made materials** such as plastic and glass fibre can mimic lead, stone or terracotta brilliantly. In addition to being cheaper than the real thing, they also weigh less and are more movable, but they age less attractively in most cases.

Hanging baskets

Used to add colour above ground level, hanging baskets can be open-mesh or solid. **Open-mesh baskets** can be planted through the sides as well as the top to create a mass of colour, but they need to be lined and they dry out quickly. Decorative designs with exposed wire are more costly.

Solid baskets are made of natural materials such as rattan, or from plastic, including 'self-watering' designs with a built-in reservoir. When planting, aim to conceal plastic types but show off natural baskets. **Liners** for open-mesh baskets are made from various materials. Choose a recycled material or coir – in natural brown or dyed green – rather than sphagnum moss gathered from the wild.

Open-mesh baskets are cheap and widely available.

Compost for containers

Potting compost is designed to retain water while remaining well aerated, ensuring that plant roots are never short of oxygen. Buy compost little and often to ensure it is fresh, store it undercover, and keep opened bags sealed to prevent them from drying out.

Soil-less or multipurpose compost

Light and clean to use, soil-less compost is excellent for short-lived seasonal displays and where weight is an issue, such as in hanging baskets. Its structure breaks down rapidly, so don't use it for long-lived container plants. Regular watering is vital as this type of compost dries out quickly and is hard to moisten again. It can also get waterlogged in wet weather, or if plants are overwatered. Fertiliser levels are short-lived, so plants will need feeding about six weeks after potting.

Soil-based compost

Composts that contain soil, or loam, have much more 'body' than soil-less types and are good for plants that will stay in tubs for more than a few months. They include the John Innes composts, of which there are several formulae, depending on the use of the compost. When planting bulbs that need good drainage, such as lilies, add a third by volume of coarse grit to the compost.

Ericaceous compost

Plants that dislike lime, such as azaleas, rhododendrons and pieris, need to be grown in ericaceous (lime-free) compost.

Compost for hanging baskets

Because baskets are exposed to the dehydrating effects of sun and wind, they benefit from a soil-less compost with water-retaining gel added. Don't use water-retaining gel in winter containers, though, as good drainage is crucial to avoid frost damage to plant roots.

Temporary containers

Seasonal and permanent plants grown in containers and raised beds rely entirely on you for their care. Feed and water regularly from late spring onwards and they will reward you with a cheerful patio display all summer and well into autumn.

A glazed terracotta pot makes a good foil for pretty daisies.

Creating a summer display

Well-planted pots and hanging baskets will cheer up the patio in summer. Plant generously for maximum impact. You can use colourful bedding to stage as bright a display as possible, or go for a colour palette, such as whites and blues.

Summer containers

Garden centres and nurseries offer a wide range of bedding and other plants for summer containers. They are often grouped by colour, so it is easy to choose those that fit a special colour scheme.

Anchor plants are central to a container, whether used alone or surrounded by smaller or trailing plants. Fuchsias are popular, but why not try something different, perhaps trained as a standard, such as Paraguay nightshade (*Solanum rantonnetii*). Succulents, like the spiky-leaved century plant (*Agave americana*), make fine anchors.

Trailing or filling plants to go with the anchors include the yellow bur marigold (*bidens*) and blue fairy fan-flower (*scaevola*). New varieties of pelargonium are bred every year, but many older kinds, especially those with aromatic leaves, are just as beautiful and easy to grow.

Use fragrance, as well as colour. Heliotrope has a delicious scent, as do easy annuals like mignonette, night-scented stocks and sweet peas, especially the older, scented varieties.

Caring for your containers

Newly bought plants for containers need to be exposed gradually to cold, windy or wet weather before they go outside. This is known as 'hardening off'. Water containers daily from late spring onwards and feed every 7-14 days during the growing season, from six weeks after planting. A tomato fertiliser is ideal.

Autumn containers

Planting containers for winter and spring decoration means taking even more care to provide good drainage. Over-wet compost can rot roots and is liable to freeze solid in winter and kill or damage the plants, particularly bulbs, so avoid using potting compost containing water-retaining gel. Mass plants closely together, as there will be little growth between autumn and spring.

Planting up

■ Put in a layer of drainage material about 5cm deep. Pieces of broken pots, or 'crocks', are ideal, but coarse gravel or chunks of broken polystyrene packing are also suitable.

■ Lay fine plastic netting or pieces of net curtain over the top of the crocks to prevent the spaces becoming clogged with compost.

■ Part-fill the container with a free-draining compost, then pack in the plants closely making sure they are at the same depth as they were growing previously.

■ Trickle compost between the rootballs so there are no air gaps.

■ Leave at least a 1cm gap between the top of the compost and the rim to allow room for watering.

■ Firm the compost lightly and water well. Stand the container on pot feet or pieces of tile so that excess water drains away freely.

Feeding

Plants grown in containers, raised beds or borders where there is a limited amount of soil need feeding regularly from late spring onwards. Liquid feeds can be given every 7-14 days, when watering, throughout the growing season. Aim to start six weeks after planting, when the fertiliser in the compost will have run out. A high-potash feed, like tomato fertiliser, promotes flowering.

Slow-release fertilisers provide all the necessary nutrients container plants need for several months or even the whole growing season – see the manufacturer's instructions. They release more nutrients as temperature and available moisture increase – just when plants need them most.

Avoid over feeding plants. It makes them grow too lush and they become disease-prone. The consequences of over feeding are more of a problem than plant starvation, especially on patios.

Watering

This is the single most important task in container gardening. More plants suffer stress through lack of water than from any other cause. Water new plants thoroughly, not only when planted but regularly later, until their root systems are developed. Once established, plants in containers and hanging baskets need watering daily.

Planting a summer container

1 Take a large pot, at least 40cm across the top and with a drainage hole. Fill to roughly two-thirds with soil-less potting compost.

2 Try out the plants in their eventual positions, placing the anchor plant centrally in the container. Then remove the plants and make a hole large enough for the anchor plant's rootball. Then place the filling and trailing plants around the edge; encourage the trailers to grow down over the sides.

3 Finally, plant the 'anchor' in the middle, add more compost between the plants and gently firm them into position. Water thoroughly.

Permanent containers

Trees, shrubs and herbaceous perennials will survive many years in containers as long as you look after them. Choose plants carefully to stand alone or use them in groups to set off displays of seasonal bedding.

Growing permanently in containers allows you to enjoy plants that require different soil and conditions from those found in your garden. Rhododendrons and pieris, for example, would not thrive in alkaline soil, but you can grow them to perfection in a pot of lime-free ericaceous compost. Spreading plants, like many bamboos, can overwhelm a small garden but look lovely in a pot and are easier to control.

This form of gardening is also extremely versatile – you can create different effects with just one permanent plant by surrounding it with temporary plants in smaller pots, changing them from season to season and from year to year.

Selecting plants

Choose trees and shrubs that are naturally slow growing, require little pruning and have appeal throughout the year. Flowering is not essential as evergreens give foliage interest in winter and provide a quiet background to summer bedding. Some, particularly conifers, have a distinct conical or rounded form; others, like box and small-leaved privets, can be trained as topiary. Standard plants are another good choice. Fuchsias, hydrangea paniculata and even wisteria can be grown this way, though these usually need permanent staking.

Don't overlook deciduous trees either. Japanese maples are shapely in and out of leaf and have wonderful foliage that changes with the seasons.

Some evergreen herbaceous perennials, like bergenias, heucheras and ornamental grasses, also make ideal subjects for a permanent container.

Choosing containers

A container must be large enough for the plant to spread its roots and grow well for at least two years. It should be sturdy, broad-based for stability and widening towards the rim, so the rootball can be slid out easily for repotting. Drainage is essential, ideally one hole 2-3cm across for every 30cm diameter of rim. Ceramic or terracotta pots must be frost-proof if they are outdoors all winter.

Planting a container

Spring is the best time to do this. Before you start, water the plant thoroughly and allow to drain. Put the pot where you want it to stand and raise it on bricks or pot feet. Put a piece of net curtain over the drainage hole to stop pests from entering or compost being washed through. Use loam-based rather than soil-less potting compost, as these retain nutrients and moisture for longer.

After planting

■ Insert supports for climbers so that the plants can grow through them from the start. By summer, the supports should be almost invisible amid the flowers.

Patio roses

It's important to select roses that suit hot, sunny patio conditions. Choose disease-resistant varieties that will flower all summer. True patio roses keep on flowering, as long as you remove the dead flowerheads throughout summer. Otherwise, make sure they don't grow too large and try to choose varieties for fragrance. Ideal varieties are 'Gentle Touch' (warm pink), 'Top Marks' (orange-red), 'Golden Sunblaze' and 'Cider Cup' (dark apricot).

Planting a tree in a container

1 Place a square of geotextile over the drainage hole and cover with 2-3cm coarse grit, for good drainage. Add some loam-based compost mixed with a little bone meal, to come about halfway up the sides of the container.

2 Position the plant centrally. Pack compost round the sides of the rootball, gently shaking the plant to eliminate air gaps. Push the compost down firmly and securely but without over compacting it.

3 Fill the container with more compost and water thoroughly. This will cause the compost to sink to the correct level. Add the mulch of your choice.

■ Protect the plants from frost, even if they are hardy. Keep some fleece handy to throw over them, but remove it in the morning as temperatures begin to rise.

■ Mulch to conserve moisture, suppress weeds and improve the pot's appearance. Use an organic material like cocoa shells, or something decorative such as pebbles, seashells or fir cones.

■ Regular watering is essential; erratic watering causes stress to the plant.

■ Feed by lightly forking in a slow-release granular fertiliser that will last all season, or water with a liquid feed at regular intervals.

In the following years

Trees and conifers don't require regular pruning, other than to remove any dead or damaged shoots, or badly growing branches. Climbers and topiary will need clipping once or twice during the growing season, and flowering shrubs require deadheading.

Leave woody plants undisturbed for two to three years before repotting, then move young plants into a larger container; you can leave more mature plants up to five years. Every spring, remove the top 5cm of old compost and replace it with fresh, mixed with a slow-release fertiliser.

In repotting years you may need to cut the roots back a little on established shrubs while they are dormant.

Climbers in containers

Climbing plants can be grown in containers, which prevents the stronger-growing varieties getting out of hand. Vigorous grape vines or wisteria trained on frames or pergolas create a shady canopy in summer, but let in more sunshine when their leaves fall in autumn. Climbing roses, too, can be used in this way, or trained over arches around the edge of the patio. Even small climbing roses, such as the bright coppery-hued 'Warm Welcome', will grow well in a large container.

Maintaining a healthy garden

A well-laid lawn should last indefinitely if properly cared for. This could well be the most important feature of your garden, so it's worth spending a little time and effort looking after it.

Mowing the lawn

Once the soil temperature rises above 5-7°C, the grass starts growing and you need to mow. The exact timing will vary from year to year, depending on the weather. Make the first cuts with the mower blades set high. The golden rule is never to reduce the length of the grass by more than a third at a single cut. As the rate of growth increases, the lawn will need more frequent mowing, and the height of cut can gradually be lowered by adjusting the blades in stages. Don't cut the grass too short, as this weakens it and exposes bare soil where moss and weeds can easily become established.

In cold areas, late spring will be the earliest you start cutting your lawn; the heavier the soil, the longer it takes to warm up. In mild areas, where the soil never freezes, you may have mown several times by late spring. Always begin by giving the shaggy lawn a light trim, with the mower blades on the highest setting.

Mowing frequency

How often you need to mow will vary according to the wetness or dryness of the season and the type of lawn you have.

■ **Fine ornamental lawns** need cutting as often as two or three times a week, to a height of about 6mm.

■ **Cut average-use lawns** once or twice a week to approximately 1cm.

■ **Hardwearing lawns**, designed for play, need one cut a week to about 2cm.

■ **For new lawns**, leave the grass slightly longer to reduce stress in dry weather.

■ **Avoid mowing too closely**, as this can reduce the vigour of the grass and make it more vulnerable to fungal diseases.

■ **Infrequent or erratic mowing** encourages moss and weeds to invade the lawn as it struggles to recover.

Protecting lawn edges

By late summer, herbaceous plants will be flopping over the edges of borders unless you have put supports in place. This will cause the edges of the lawn to turn brown as well as making them difficult to mow.

Insert either purpose-made support frames or twiggy 'pea sticks' to pull plants back, or use canes and string to keep leafy plants off the lawn. Alternatively, lay a hard 'mowing edge' between lawn and border.

Feeding your lawn

Regular mowing saps the strength of the grass, especially if you use a grass box, so you should start feeding your lawn in spring, once it has started to grow.

Types of lawnmowers

■ **Cylinder mowers** cut the grass with a vertically rotating cylinder of blades and a fixed bottom blade. They make a very fine finish, and are usually fitted with front and rear rollers and a grass box.

■ **Rotary mowers** have a horizontal blade that rotates at high speed and cuts mainly by slashing the grass off. The most basic ones don't collect the grass, but the more sophisticated types have grass boxes, and also a roller for giving a striped effect to the newly mown lawn.

■ **Self-propelled petrol mowers** can take some of the effort out of grass cutting, but must be capable of being overridden to hand operated if necessary – for example, in tight or awkward corners.

Scarifier

Lawn rake

Aerator

- **Scarifier** Removes surface debris and dead grass. It's pushed over the lawn, rotating a series of tines or blades that rake through the grass.
- **Lawn rake** With spring tines arranged in a fan shape, this tool is ideal for raking out moss, leaves and removing surface debris.
- **Fertiliser spreader** A drum on wheels that is pushed along, while rotating blades below the drum spray out the granular fertiliser for up to 1m on either side.
- **Aerator** This introduces air into the soil and aerates roots. It consists of a frame of tines or blades. These are pushed into the ground all over the lawn. Those with hollow tines remove tiny cores of soil that can be replaced with a top dressing or sand.

Fertiliser spreader

All spring lawn feeds are high in nitrogen to promote rapid, green leaf growth. If you use a powdered or granular fertiliser, water it in if no rain falls within 48 hours of applying it. You can apply liquid feeds through a hose diluter or, for small lawns, use a watering can and dilute the solution according to the manufacturer's instructions.

Lawn health

To stay green and healthy, grass needs more attention than simply mowing. Remove moss and dead grass debris and fallen leaves and aerate your lawn.

To control moss successfully, you must tackle the underlying causes such as shade, compacted soil and poor drainage. Moss can also build up in wet winters on otherwise healthy lawns and, if left untreated, it will smother and eventually kill the grass. The use of a lawn sand, that is a combined moss and weedkiller with added fertiliser, saves time and is ideal for busy gardeners. As this product feeds the grass, it will recover relatively quickly and grow over the gaps left by the dead moss.

Choose a day when there is heavy dew so that the chemicals stick to the moss and weed leaves. The moss and other weeds turn alarmingly black within a week, but wait until the moss goes brown, which means that it's completely dead, before raking. Reapply lawn sand to any moss patches that go green again. Dispose of the dead moss, but don't put it in the compost bin, because of chemical residues.

Remove annual weeds before they set seed because seeds can stay in the soil for years and may germinate whenever the soil is dug over. Perennial weeds need to be caught early and removed before their root systems have a chance to spread.

A weed is defined as any plant growing in the wrong place. Many native wild flowers are classed as weeds when growing among border plants or vegetables, but are welcomed in a wild-flower meadow. Conversely, tulips would not look out of place in a border, but would be quite unacceptable – and therefore technically weeds – in a native wild-flower meadow.

Organic methods of control

The best way to control weeds is to keep on top of them. If you start with clean soil, you can hoe off or pull out all seedling weeds as they appear so they never get the chance to become established. Mulching with chipped bark, cocoa shell, stone chippings and gravel, especially if a weed-barrier sheet or black polythene is laid on the soil first, will slow down weed regrowth, but seedlings eventually appear in mulches and must be removed immediately. The tops of young weeds are easily pulled out or hoed off, or you can singe them with a gas flame gun.

Established perennial weeds can be more difficult to eliminate. If you are prepared to wait, covering the soil with heavy-gauge black polythene will smother the majority of weeds within 12 months, but some stubborn ones, like ground elder, Japanese knotweed

---

Common annual weeds

Chickweed (1) A low mat up to 30cm across. Hoe or hand weed to remove stems, which can reroot.

Cleavers (2) Hoe in early spring before it seeds in summer. Stems reach several feet and are covered with sticky hairs. Adult plants are difficult to disentangle from other plants.

Groundsel (3) Hoe in dry weather when small. Seeds will germinate throughout the year. Adult weed produces small, yellow, dandelion-like flowers and grows 23-40cm.

Hairy bittercress (4) Can flower and set seed very quickly so hoe seedlings immediately – from late spring to autumn. Flower spikes reach about 20cm from small leaf rosettes.

Dead nettle, red (5) Hoe seedlings that appear in spring and autumn. Mature plants grow to 45cm and produce red or purple flowers all summer.

Fat hen (6) Hoe seedlings that appear throughout the growing season. Hand weed older plants which have triangular leaves and reach 90cm tall. Seed is long-lived.

Ivy-leaved speedwell (7) Hoe seedlings that appear over winter starting in October. By April sprawling stems are covered in tiny pale blue flowers. Seed dispersed by ants.

Knotgrass (8) Hoe or hand weed seedlings in spring and early summer. If left, plants will grow to 60cm and flower any time between July and October.

Common perennial weeds

Bindweed (1) Hoe often or use a systemic weedkiller in spring before plants climb and wind around other plants. White or pink flowers in summer.

Dandelion (2) Hoe seedlings that appear from spring. Large plants need to be dug out or killed with a spot weedkiller. Take action before the plant sets seed.

Dock, broad leaved (3) Seedlings appear throughout the growing season. Hoe them or dig them out when they are bigger. Otherwise spot treat with a systemic weedkiller. Older plants can reach up to 90cm tall.

Greater plantain (4) Hoe out seedlings when they appear in spring and autumn. Flowers in its first year. Plants can reach 30cm. Seed is long-lived.

Couch grass (5) Hoe out seedlings when they appear in summer. Once plants are established use systemic weed-killer. Plants can reach 75cm tall.

Japanese knotweed (6) A real problem weed once it's established. In the early stages it can be dug out. Use a systemic weedkiller on mature plants. Repeat as necessary.

Creeping buttercup (7) Hoe seedlings from spring to autumn. Once established, dig out by hand, or spot treat with systemic weedkiller.

Stinging nettle (8) Hoe out young seedlings which appear throughout the growing season. Dig out older plants, or spot treat with systemic weedkiller. Leave some to attract wildlife. Seed is long-lived.

and couch grass, may take much longer. Digging them out is quicker, but some weeds, like bindweed and horsetail, are difficult to remove entirely as every little piece left behind will regrow.

Using weedkillers

Weedkillers, or herbicides, used correctly, are a highly efficient way of removing weeds. Selective weedkillers eliminate a certain category of weeds, and are generally found in lawn treatments containing the chemicals 2,4-D and mecoprop-p. Soil-applied herbicides, such as dichlobenil and sodium chlorate, kill roots and emerging growth, and are usually restricted to path weed control or around woody plants where you wish to keep the soil clean for a long period. Foliage-applied weedkillers either kill weeds by contact, like paraquat and diquat, or by translocation, when the plant absorbs the chemical through the leaf and takes it down to the roots – like glyphosate. This weedkiller is widely used because it's highly efficient if applied correctly and, once the weeds are dead, the ground can be replanted immediately. There are also woody plant and stump killers, such as ammonium sulphamate, which is used to kill and rot off the stump when a tree is felled.

Take care! Read the instructions carefully. Make sure you have the right product for your job and apply it strictly according to the manufacturer's guidelines. Always apply weedkillers on a still day and keep animals and children well away for the recommended time. Keep a watering can or sprayer specifically for weed control. Store chemicals in a safe place and never decant from their original containers.

You will need to feed your plants for them to thrive. Intensive cultivation takes more out of the soil than it puts back. The situation is compounded if you remove plant debris that would otherwise rot and return nutrients to the soil.

Fertilisers

All your garden plants – from lawn to container specimens – need feeding in order to perform at their best. In a garden, plants are grown unnaturally close together and when they do die down, we tend to remove the debris – which therefore gives nothing back to the soil naturally.

You can feed plants with concentrated fertilisers or organic manures, or a mixture of the two.

■ **Manures** are generally regarded as those with an organic origin, such as dung, garden compost and leaf-mould, which break down into humus. They must be well rotted.

■ **Fertilisers** provide little or no humus, but have elements in a concentrated form that supplement the soil's own nutrients.

If you are new to gardening, you are best off using bulky manures such as garden compost and farmyard manure, or balanced fertilisers according to manufacturer's instructions. If you use 'straight feeds' (those containing one nutritional element only) you risk causing an imbalance of nutrients in the soil.

Types of fertiliser

Both artificial and organic fertilisers supplement the three principal nutrients essential to plant growth: nitrogen, phosphorus and potassium. These chemicals can be bought separately (such as sulphate of ammonia) or combined in a general-purpose fertiliser like Growmore.

■ **Nitrogen** produces growth; too little results in small yellow leaves and lack of vigour.

■ **Phosphorus** is important to seedlings and roots. Too little turns leaves dull purple and slows down growth.

Inorganic fertilisers

These fertilisers provide individual plant nutrients in a concentrated and generally readily accessible form: phosphate of potash; rock phosphate; sulphate of ammonia; sulphate of magnesium (Epsom salts); sulphate of potash; superphosphate of lime.

■ **Potassium** encourages flowering and fruiting; it also improves resistance to pests and diseases and hardens tissues.

■ **Other nutrients**, called trace elements, are also necessary in tiny quantities for healthy growth, and are present in a number of fertiliser formulations.

Fertilisers are available in solid or liquid form, or as foliar feeds, applied with a watering can or plant sprayer and rapidly absorbed through the leaves. Wear gloves when handling fertilisers and apply according to the manufacturer's instructions.

Gardening the organic way

Organic gardening is gardening with the wider environment in mind. It relies on natural methods to control pests and to build up the fertility of the soil. Organic gardening recycles farm and garden wastes rather than disposing of them in ways that would pollute the environment.

Enriching the soil

The starting point for effective organic gardening is to create soil that holds moisture but drains well and encourages extensive root growth. It will provide plants with a balanced, slow-release diet to promote steady growth. The plants will then be less prone to attack by pests and diseases than chemically fed plants.

Organic mulches and fertilisers

The following are of organic origin and supply nutrients and/or improve soil texture and fertility: composted bark; bone meal; coir; dried blood; farmyard manure; fish, blood and bone; garden compost; hoof and horn meal; leaf-mould; mushroom compost; peat (use as a last resort because of environmental issues); seaweed meal; wood ash.

Soil improvers

To improve the soil, use garden compost and leaf-mould, supplemented with brought-in ingredients such as animal manure and extra autumn leaves. Do not use manures derived from intensive farming systems because of the higher levels of food additives, antibiotics and other chemicals. Instead, opt for garden compost, well-rotted manure, mushroom compost, hay, seaweed, cocoa shells and grass cuttings. These are all rich in nutrients and can be dug into the soil before planting.

Low-nutrient materials, such as straw, leaf-mould, composted bark and prunings chopped up in a shredder, may be applied at any time of the year and in any quantity.

Organic soil improvers can be used either as a surface mulch or mixed with the top 15cm layer of soil. A mulch acts as an insulating layer and should be applied to warm, wet soil only. Unrotted soil improvers, such as hay, straw, seaweed and grass cuttings, can be composted first or added straight to the garden. If not composted, use as a mulch.

Hungry roses will benefit from a top dressing of well-rotted manure, applied to warm, damp soil every spring.

All plants need enough water to survive, which means that artificial watering is usually necessary during dry spells. With reserves often running low in summer, it makes sense to use water as wisely as possible in the garden, both for environmental reasons and to save money on metered supplies.

Conserving water

Well-established plants in the ground should be able to survive all but severe drought without extra water, so concentrate watering on those plants that must not be allowed to dry out. The key to successful plant survival starts way back at the soil preparation and planting stage, with the addition of organic matter to the soil; this improves its water-holding capacity as it acts like a sponge. You should also 'lock in' valuable moisture by mulching the ground every spring to reduce evaporation from the soil. Apply a 5-8cm layer of chipped bark, well-rotted manure or garden compost; and if you garden on free-draining, fast-drying soil, choose drought-tolerant plants.

Watering techniques

■ **In hot weather**, water in the evening or early morning, which is when less moisture is lost by evaporation, and when plants can

Priority plants

In dry weather, concentrate on watering those plants that need it most.

- **New plants** Don't allow these to dry out during their first year, as they will not have established enough of a root system to take up sufficient moisture.
- **New lawns** Whether they have been made from seed or turf, new lawns need to be kept moist for several months until established. Fine lawns also need watering regularly. Existing general-purpose lawns can be left to their own devices – despite turning brown, they will green up quickly once rain arrives.
- **Annuals and newly sown seed** These must not dry out for the first few weeks after planting; after that you can get away with an occasional soaking during dry spells, except for thirsty plants like sweet peas that prefer regular watering.
- **Plants in containers** You will need to water these frequently, even daily, in summer.
- **Vegetables** To produce good crops, all vegetables benefit from regular watering, particularly leafy vegetables such as salad crops and spinach, and those with large or succulent fruits such as tomatoes, cucumbers, squashes or courgettes.
- **Soft fruit** Strawberries and raspberries need watering while the fruit is developing.

take up water more efficiently. This also avoids the danger of water-splashed leaves becoming scorched in bright sunshine.

■ **In cooler seasons,** water early in the day so that the foliage then has a chance to dry out, as moist leaves provide an attractive environment for disease.

■ **Water the soil,** not the plant. During the growing season, always give plants a thorough soaking – not just a sprinkling.

Watering patios

Plants in pots may not receive adequate natural watering, especially in summer. Add water-retaining gels to composts for summer displays and line wire hanging baskets with polythene. Large, non-porous pots dry out more slowly than small terracotta ones. Self-watering containers reduce the need to water, but don't use them in winter as they can become waterlogged.

Patio watering systems

You can cut your workload dramatically by installing a watering system; the inclusion of a timer makes the system completely automatic. A basic design consists of a rigid hose running to the area to be watered. Flexible microbore tubing travels from the hose to the containers, delivering water to each pot by means of an attached drip nozzle. The hose itself connects to a tap which you turn on manually unless you fit a timer. Watering systems are perfect for containers as the water is delivered slowly and gently.

Using water-retaining gel

Choose soil-based compost for all permanent plants as it's best at retaining water. You can improve the water-holding capacity of soil-less compost by using water-retaining gel, made up of granules that swell to many times their own size when wet. Mix just a small quantity of the dry granules into the compost before potting – or you can buy compost that already contains the gel. Make sure you water frequently, because once the gel has given up its store of moisture, the compost dries out very quickly. Do not use gel for containers that will be left outside in autumn, winter or early spring, as the compost will become too wet and cold.

Recycling and saving water

- Collect rainwater in a butt.
- Use recycled or 'grey' water from baths and sinks on the garden, but don't recycle water from washing machines and dishwashers, as these use strong detergents.

Before you wage all out war on garden bugs, remember that many beneficial creatures need a supply of what we consider pests to survive. If you got rid of every slug and snail, for example, you would seriously impair the diet of some birds. Unless pests are wreaking havoc in your garden, then leave them be.

Garden pests and diseases are not nearly as common as you would think from looking at the array of potions on the relevant shelves of the garden centre. Correct planting, good maintenance and the choice of resistant varieties will cut down problems to a minimum, and only using chemicals when absolutely necessary encourages natural controls to build up. Sometimes, though, you have to act.

myclobutanil. Better still, grow a resistant variety such as 'Invicta'.

■ **Aphids – greenfly and blackfly (2)** Suck the sap from plant to weaken and distort plants, and can also spread diseases. Spray with insecticidal soap, pyrethrum or derris as soon as spotted. They secrete a sticky substance (honeydew) that can cause sooty mould. This can be washed off with a weak solution of detergent if it becomes serious.

Controlling pests and diseases

Occasionally, even in the best-maintained gardens, some bugs and blights may occur. The following are those you are most likely to encounter.

■ **American gooseberry mildew (1)** Leaves and fruit are covered in a brown, felty substance in summer. Remove and burn diseased shoots and spray plant with

■ **Apple canker (3)** A serious disease of apples and pears. Remove affected shoots and small branches completely, cut out the cankerous area of larger branches completely and treat with a wound paint.

■ **Brown rot (4)** Mainly affects apples, pears and plums. Infected fruit turns brown and rots. Remove as soon as noticed – don't compost. Clear up infected windfalls and take off any mummified fruits after the leaves have dropped in autumn. Be careful not to store fruit showing signs of brown rot.

■ **Cabbage root fly (5)** The maggots eat the roots of members of the cabbage family, including wallflowers and stocks. First signs are when the plant looks stunted, turns a bluish tint and starts to wilt. Use brassica collars or plant through crop protection fabric, pieces of linoleum or carpet underlay.

■ **Carrot fly (6)** Maggots eat the roots. Foliage turns red and stunted, then yellow and dies off. Grow quick-maturing varieties early or late in the season, sow thinly to avoid excessive thinning, and thin as little as possible. Otherwise grow in tubs or raised beds at least 45cm above ground level.

■ **Club root** A serious disease of members of the cabbage family, including ornamental species, causing swollen, distorted roots. Plants lose vigour and wilt in sunny weather. Don't grow these types of plants for several years where club root has become a bad problem, although potting on cabbages and similar plants into large plant pots and planting out when they are well established and have a large and robust root system may overcome the infection.

■ **Cutworms (8)** Sever the stems of young plants at ground level. Hoe round plants and remove grubs brought to the surface.

■ **Gooseberry sawfly** Green caterpillars with black spots, 2cm long, strip the leaves off

1 American gooseberry mildew 2 Aphids (greenfly and blackfly)
3 Apple canker 4 Brown rot 5 Cabbage root fly 6 Carrot fly
7 Caterpillars 8 Cutworms

■ **Caterpillars (7)** Eat leaves and destroy plants if not checked. Crush small outbreaks by hand, including eggs, as soon as noticed (wearing gloves to prevent skin irritation). Spray bad infestations with derris.

■ **Chafer grubs** Feed on the roots of many garden plants. Remove any grubs brought to the surface by cultivation. Biological controls are available by mail order, on the internet and from some garden centres.

gooseberry bushes. Spray with derris or pyrethrum at the first sign of damage.

■ **Grey mould (botrytis)** Many kinds of plants are affected by this disease, which is worse in cold, damp weather. Clear up old plant material and remove affected leaves, flowers and stems. Take care not to overwater or wet the foliage too much during these conditions.

■ **Leatherjackets** Cause bare patches in lawns and can damage the roots of herbaceous perennials. Biological controls are available on the internet and from many garden centres. Water affected patches in grass and cover overnight with black polythene; the leatherjackets will come to the surface and can be swept up. Regular cultivation will get rid of them in the vegetable garden.

■ **Lily beetle (1)** Bright red beetles and their slime-covered grubs can seriously damage flowers and leaves of members of

■ **Powdery mildew (3)** Different strains of this fungal disease affect different plants – including roses, Michaelmas daisies, apples and strawberries. Spray with a proprietary fungicide (mancozeb) at fortnightly intervals once the disease appears.

■ **Onion fly** Maggots eat the roots of onions and kill the plants. Grow onion sets rather than raising from seed. Firm the soil around the bulbs and hoe between rows regularly. Burn infested plants and dig over ground to expose dormant pupae to frost and birds.

■ **Pea moth (4)** Causes maggoty peas. Grow a resistant variety (see a seed catalogue for suggestions); otherwise sow a quick-maturing variety early or late in the season.

the lily family, including *Convallaria* (lily of the valley). Mainly found in the south of England, especially Surrey. Pick them off as soon as spotted. Control bad infestations by spraying with imidacloprid.

■ **Peach leaf curl (2)** A rain-borne fungal disease affecting all members of the peach family (almonds, nectarines). Tent wall-trained trees with a roof of polythene from late autumn until early spring.

■ **Raspberry beetle** Adults eat the flowers and the grubs cause maggoty fruit. Spray with derris when the first fruits turn pink.

■ **Rose black spot (5)** Can defoliate bushes if bad enough. Buy disease-resistant varieties, clear up all fallen leaves and prune hard in autumn, removing all leaves. Spray at the first signs with a proprietary fungicide and repeat at fortnightly intervals throughout the season. Spray preventatively before the disease occurs if bushes have been badly infected the previous season.

■ **Red spider mite (6)** Can be a problem in hot, dry situations. The leaves are covered with an unsightly, dusty-looking web. Control by misting daily with water; derris may have some effect.

■ **Rust** Hollyhocks seem especially susceptible to rust, in which orange blisters appear on the underside of leaves, usually from late summer. Spray with a proprietary fungicide at fortnightly intervals.

■ **Scale insects (7)** May cover the stems of certain, usually woody plants and suck sap. First signs are that the plant starts to weaken. Scrape off with a thumb nail or

problem, as they eat roots and can kill a wide variety of plants if not dealt with quickly. Water containers with imidacloprid in spring and autumn, or use a biological control. Improve drainage as the problem is worse in damp conditions, and mulch with pea gravel, stone chippings or chipped bark.

■ **Viruses** Plants are affected by many viruses. Some viruses are actively encouraged by breeders to create special effects, like streaked petals in tulips; many plants can be infected with certain viruses without any obvious effect. Other viruses can cause plants to weaken gradually; there is no control or cure, and affected specimens should be dug up and destroyed.

spray with imidacloprid to kill the insects – the remains will drop off in time.

■ **Slugs and snails** Cause serious damage to a wide range of garden plants. Slugs can be treated with a biological control, otherwise use slug pellets according to manufacturer's instructions or an organic control like a copper-based product or aluminium sulphate.

■ **Vine weevils (8)** Adult weevils bite small notches in leaf edges. The grubs are the real

1 Lily beetle **2** Peach leaf curl **3** Powdery mildew **4** Pea moth
5 Rose black spot **6** Red spider mite **7** Scale insects **8** Vine weevils

■ **Woolly aphid** Aphids form colonies and secrete a white, waxy waterproof coating that is resistant to insecticidal sprays. They affect apples and related ornamental trees and shrubs. The best method of control is to spray off with a high pressure jet of water, but the bugs will eventually return.

Some cutting back in the garden is always necessary, even with new planting. To do the job properly, it helps to understand the need for it, and what may happen if the job is neglected.

There are three main categories of cutting back – cutting down perennials; clipping hedges and small, dense shrubs; and pruning trees, shrubs, roses and fruit.

Cutting back perennials

Most herbaceous perennials are cut back in autumn, to remove dead stems and tidy the plant so it does not give pests and diseases a chance to overwinter in them. But if you like the effect of frost and snow on, say, dead grasses and stalks bearing seed heads, then cut these back in spring. It's also better to cut back slightly tender evergreen perennials, such as penstemons, in spring, as freezing weather can damage cut stems and cause the plants to die-back completely.

Cutting back perennials can be done either with secateurs or shears. Using secateurs is slower, but it's easy to collect the rubbish as you go. Shears get the job done faster, but the bits scatter and must be raked up.

Trimming hedges and dense shrubs

Dense shrubs, like hebes, heathers and lavender, need regular cutting back to extend their life and keep them tidy. Topiary specimens are treated in the same way. The most suitable tool for this is a sharp pair of shears. Hedges also need regular trimming, from an early age, to form and maintain a good shape. Shorter runs of hedging can be kept in good order with hedging shears, but

The correct pruning cut

Pruning cuts through the bark, which is what protects a plant from disease. The cleaner the cut, the faster the wound will dry and heal, so it's important to keep tools sharp, and avoid ragged cuts and torn bark. Plants have natural defences against injury concentrated in certain places, such as in the joint where bud or leaf grows. Cutting close to this point helps the wound to heal quickly.

Always prune just above a bud, sloping the cut to direct water away from the bud.

A correctly pruned cut (below) will heal quickly, whereas using blunt secateurs produces a ragged cut and torn bark, which will take longer to heal.

Where buds are in pairs on opposite sides of the stem (above), cut straight across, no more than 5mm above the buds.

Trimming a privet hedge

1 Clip the sides of the hedge first, working from the bottom up. Gently sweep away the trimmings as you go.

2 Trim the sides to an upright profile or, more traditionally, to a slight batter (an inward lean) so that light can more easily reach the base of the hedge.

3 Clip the top to a string line. To ensure a consistent level, trim a wide hedge in two stages, working to the middle from each side.

long ones are best clipped with a hedge-trimmer. The number of cuts a year depends on what the hedge is made of, but even slow-growing ones need clipping annually to keep them thick. A few hedging plants, in particular laurel, should be pruned with secateurs rather than clipped, as the cut leaves turn brown and fall off. However, if you have a very long laurel hedge, this is impractical, and the hedge soon greens up again when the new growth appears.

Pruning shrubby and woody plants

Some woody plants are pruned to encourage the formation of either flowers or fruit – this is the case with roses (page 80), soft fruit (page 96), and apples and pears (see page 97). In addition, the removal of dead and unwanted wood also keeps trees and bushes healthy and a good shape.

Most ornamental shrubs don't need regular pruning to do well, although in time they get over large, untidy and overcrowded if not cut back periodically (page 86). Those grown for brightly coloured young foliage or coloured bark do need regular pruning for best effect; this usually involves cutting back with secateurs or loppers to a few centimetres above ground level, or to the main trunk if trained as an ornamental tree, just before the leaves appear in spring.

True ornamental trees (as opposed to shrubs trained on a single stem as trees for small spaces) are pruned in their early years by removing the lower branches to form a trunk. Apart from that, most healthy trees should not need pruning at all, except to encourage attractive foliage – the label when you buy it will tell you if this is the case.

If a tree needs cutting back because it's too large for the space where it's growing, it was the wrong choice in the first place. You may be able to solve this problem by removing whole branches with a bow or pruning saw. Consult a tree surgeon if you are at all unsure. 'Snip-pruning' – clipping back the ends of the branches – is rarely successful and will affect flowering and overall appearance. It will also encourage longer and stronger shoots that need cutting back very frequently. You may decide that it's best to cut your losses, remove the tree and replace it with something more suitable.

	Late winter (end of January/beginning of February)	Early spring (late February/March)
General jobs	Wash pots and seed trays; order seeds from catalogues; plan changes; dig empty ground.	Finish digging; prepare ground for sowing and planting.
Lawns	Lay turf; cut existing lawns, with blades set high if grass starts to grow in mild spells.	Lay turf; prepare ground for seeding; treat moss; top existing lawns if necessary.
Hard landscaping	Lay new patios and drives in suitable weather; check existing areas for damage and repair if necessary.	Lay new patios and drives, repair existing ones.
Fences and walls	Build new walls, except in frosty weather; erect fences; check fences for stability, especially after high winds.	Erect new walls and fences, check and repair existing ones if necessary.
Paths	Lay new paths; repair existing ones.	Lay new paths and repair existing ones; treat weeds with path weedkiller.
Containers	Check winter containers for moisture, water if dry, and check drainage holes if too wet; clean empty pots and baskets.	Feed with liquid flower food as plants start to bloom; water in dry weather.
Annuals	Inspect winter pansies for aphids at base of stems; spray with insecticide if necessary.	Thin autumn-sown hardy annuals; prepare seedbed for spring-sown ones; order plug plants.
Perennials	Plant containerised perennials in mild spells; check base of established plants for snails; cut back tops.	Split overgrown clumps; finish cutting back old growth; plant new ones; check for slugs and snails.
Alpines	Check for early growth of weeds and remove if necessary.	Construct new alpine beds and weed existing ones.
Bulbs	Support narcissi with twiggy prunings if they start blowing over; divide snowdrop clumps after flowering and replant.	Feed spring bulbs.
Roses	Start or continue pruning in mild areas; plant new roses if not frosty.	Finish planting bare-root roses; apply fungicide; continue pruning; weed beds, top-dress with rose fertiliser, and mulch.
Shrubs	Plant new shrubs in open weather; move established shrubs.	Cut back late flowerers; weed, fertilise and mulch; cut back hard shrubs grown for coloured bark or young leaf colour.
Climbers	Tie in stems loosened by the wind.	Prune large-flowered clematis; train plants on supports; feed with slow-release fertiliser.
Trees	Prune deciduous trees if not frosty; check stakes and ties on young trees; plant new trees.	Finish pruning deciduous trees; complete planting bare-root ones; feed young stock with fertiliser.
Conifers	Knock snow off branches to prevent damage.	Feed with balanced fertiliser.
Vegetables	Harvest winter crops. Cover brassicas (cabbage, broccoli, etc.) with fleece or netting to prevent bird damage.	Make seedbeds; harvest overwintering crops; sow early peas and broad beans.
Fruit	Plant new trees and bushes; prune apples and pears; protect bush fruit buds from birds.	Finish pruning apples and pears and the planting of bare-root plants; continue planting containerised ones; fertilise.

Spring (April)	Late spring (May)	Early summer (June)
Buy potting compost and new pots and seed trays if necessary.	Clean plant pots, seed trays and containers as they become empty.	Make compost of all garden waste unless diseased.
Sow or turf new lawns, cut existing ones regularly; apply summer lawn food, treat weeds; repair patches and edges.	Finish turfing and seeding; water new lawns if dry; apply fertiliser; treat weeds; mow regularly.	Mow regularly; feed if necessary; remove weeds.
This is a good month for starting all hard landscaping projects.	Continue new projects and necessary work on existing areas.	As Late spring.
Construct fences and walls; paint metal; treat fences with preservative.	Treat unplanted fences with preservative; erect new walls and fences.	As Late spring.
Continue applying path weedkillers; start or continue new projects.	Make new paths, repair existing ones and top-up gravel ones as necessary.	As Late spring.
Feed and water spring containers regularly; plant up summer hanging baskets in the greenhouse.	Discard and compost spring container plants when faded; continue to feed and water later and permanent ones.	Remove spring bedding; plant up summer containers; hang baskets; tidy plants; feed and water regularly.
Sow hardy annuals outdoors and half-hardy ones in greenhouse/conservatory; pot on plug plants as they arrive.	Harden off home-grown half-hardy annuals; thin out outdoor-sown hardy ones.	Deadhead hardy annuals; plant out half-hardy annuals and keep well watered; deal with slugs and snails.
Divide and plant the less hardy; continue planting container-grown types; apply fertiliser; remove early weeds.	Plant container-raised plants; stake tall perennials; cut back spring-flowering varieties as blooms fade.	Keep taller varieties well staked; cut back early flowerers; deadhead repeat flowerers; control slugs and snails.
Plant new alpines; weed beds and containers; top up grit or pea gravel mulch; check for slugs and snails.	Plant up sinks and troughs; cut back early flowering, trailing types; water in the dry; pull out weed seedlings.	Continue planting alpines; treat slugs and snails; water troughs and sinks regularly.
Remove dead heads (leaving stalks and leaves); feed if not already done.	Continue deadheading spring bulbs; cut back foliage after six weeks; plant summer types.	Deadhead later-flowering spring bulbs; clear foliage as it dies off; continue planting summer bulbs.
Complete pruning; apply fertiliser and mulch; spray for disease; check young shoots for aphids and then treat.	Water new plants regularly; watch for pests and diseases.	Deadhead regularly; keep new bushes well watered; check for pests and diseases and spray if necessary.
Prune early flowering shrubs after flowering; feed and mulch; plant container-grown shrubs.	Plant container-grown shrubs; prune early flowering kinds after flowering; water newly planted specimens if dry.	Continue pruning shrubs after flowering.
Tie into supports; check for disease and spray if necessary.	Continue tying in new shoots; water young climbers against walls and fences regularly.	As Late spring.
Plant container-grown specimens and young, bare-root evergreen trees.	Check young trees and remove dead shoots if necessary.	Check ties on young trees in case they need loosening; water newly planted trees thoroughly in hot, dry weather.
Trim dwarf conifers, but leave the larger until after the nesting season; water and mist newly planted conifers if dry.	Keep young specimens well watered.	As Late spring.
Sow hardy vegetables; sow half-hardy ones in greenhouse; harvest over-wintering crops, dig over and fertilise.	Sow summer vegetables; plant out half-hardy after frosts; thin seedlings and water in; make frame for runner beans.	Thin crops; sow for succession; pick mature crops; water in and give weekly liquid feed; plant half-hardy vegetables.
Plant containerised fruit trees and bushes; check strawberries for slugs and snails; apply fertiliser.	Mulch strawberries with plant protection fabric or straw; protect from birds; water new trees, bushes and canes.	Protect soft fruit against birds; water soft fruit and young top fruit; harvest soft fruit; thin overcrowded fruit.

	Mid/late summer (July to early September)	**Autumn** (mid September to early October)
General jobs	Start designing parts of the garden; spray uncultivated land with glyphosate weedkiller; clear unwanted plants.	Send for seed and plant catalogues; start digging vacant ground and preparing for new projects.
Lawns	Water new lawns in dry spells; leave grass long in periods of drought; apply lawn food; prepare soil for new lawns.	Apply an autumn fertiliser if not already done; seed or turf new lawns, and repair existing ones; gradually reduce mowing.
Hard landscaping	Start completing ongoing jobs before the cold weather.	As Late summer. Treat paved areas with a patio cleaner to get rid of moss, lichen and green algae.
Fences and walls	Erect new fences and walls before winter; treat timber with preservative; check fence posts for stability.	Repair before winter; erect new ones; apply preservative to dry wood.
Paths	Make new paths before winter for ease of access to all parts of garden.	As Hard landscaping.
Containers	Continue to feed and water; deadhead regularly; remove slugs and snails.	Clear out finished plants; refill with new compost and replant with spring bedding; plant up winter baskets.
Annuals	Pull up finished hardy annuals; feed and water half-hardy annuals; buy plug plants; pot on for planting out later.	Clear when untidy and fork over ground; add bone meal and replace with spring bedding or permanent plants.
Perennials	Cut back and deadhead; control slugs and snails.	Cut down old stems; clear dead foliage; fork over bare earth; dress with bone meal; plant container-grown perennials.
Alpines	Tidy established plants and plant new ones; check mulch and top up with grit or gravel; watch for slugs and snails.	Tidy up old leaves and stems; check for slugs and snails.
Bulbs	Feed summer bulbs; buy narcissus bulbs as they become available; plant all spring-flowering bulbs except tulips.	Plant spring bulbs (not tulips), adding bone meal; in colder areas, lift summer bulbs, clean and store in a cool place.
Roses	Fertlise; water new bushes; check for pests and diseases; deadhead; remove flowered shoots on ramblers.	Continue deadheading and spraying for disease; plant container-grown bushes.
Shrubs	Finish pruning early flowering shrubs; water young specimens in drought; shorten back extra-long young shoots.	Neaten untidy growth; plant container shrubs and bare-root evergreens; fork in old mulch; top-dress with bone meal.
Climbers	Remove some flowered shoots; prune wall shrubs; water young plants well; train and tie in new growth.	Cut back untidy shoots; tie in new ones; top-dress soil with bone meal; fork in lightly; plant container-grown climbers.
Trees	Water young trees well during prolonged dry weather; remove dead and dying growth.	Check stakes and replace if broken; replace ties if too tight; start cutting out unwanted wood.
Conifers	Trim conifers once the birds have finished nesting; water young plants.	Plant new conifers and move existing ones; stake taller ones into the head if they are likely to suffer from wind rock.
Vegetables	Start planting winter and spring plants; water; fertilise weekly; sow a late crop of salad leaves; plant winter vegetables.	Clear pea and bean tops and other rubbish; plant spring cabbage; protect brassicas from birds.
Fruit	Pick soft fruit; prune cane fruit after harvesting; harvest early top fruit; water new plants; prepare for new planting.	Prune soft fruit bushes; top-dress bare soil with bone meal; plant container-grown fruit trees and bushes.

Late autumn (mid October to early November)	Early/mid winter (mid November to early December)	Midwinter (mid December to mid January)
Clean canes after use; tidy garden shed; clean and oil tools for winter storage.	Clear up fallen leaves from lawns and plants; use time to plan ahead.	Only work on the garden if not frozen or flooded; in bad weather use the time to plan ahead.
Continue turfing during fine weather; only mow existing lawns if they continue to grow.	Lay turf or dig ground for new lawns in good weather.	Dig ground for new lawns in good weather.
Keep paving algae-free with a patio cleaner; complete on-going projects before winter.	Cover wet concrete and new brickwork with old sacks if frost forecast; remove algae from paving and concrete.	Plan new projects for spring.
Renew fence posts and panels if necessary; concrete-in post spikes in exposed situations.	Repair wind-damaged fences before the damage gets worse; dismantle unsafe structures.	Dismantle unsafe structures after wind and erect temporary barriers until the weather improves.
Treat slippery paths with a path cleaner; clear weeds from cracks and gravel; trim grass from edges.	Make good holes caused by frost; treat icy paths with salt; keep free from algae, lichen and moss.	Keep free from algae, lichen and moss; plan a new feature for the coming summer.
Continue planting winter containers; repair or replace faulty hanging-basket brackets and wall fixings.	Wrap permanent containers in two layers of bubble wrap if frost forecast; protect tender plants with fleece.	Wrap permanent containers in bubble wrap if prolonged freezing forecast; protect tender patio plants with fleece.
Finish clearing summer annuals; continue replanting with spring bedding or permanent plants.	Check autumn-sown hardy annual seedlings for bird or slug damage; net and scatter a few slug pellets.	Make a new year resolution to try something new.
Continue cutting back; plant new container-grown and bare-root perennials.	See Late autumn. Only plant if weather is mild and soil not too wet; check new plants have not been loosened by frost.	Check that new plants have not been loosened by frost.
Remove tree leaves immediately if they have fallen onto the plants.	Keep beds, troughs and sinks clear of leaves and rubbish; check that new plants have not been loosened by frost.	Make sure the drainage holes of sinks and troughs have not become blocked.
Continue planting spring-flowering bulbs and start planting tulips; complete lifting summer bulbs in colder areas.	Finish planting spring bulbs; check stored bulbs for mouse damage; ensure drainage holes of troughs not blocked.	Protect buried bulbs from mice/squirrels with chicken wire; cover spring bulbs with cloches; remove dead blooms.
Plant bare-root and container bushes; prune; shorten top growth in cold areas; dress with bone meal, renew mulch.	Plant new roses; if frosty, put bare-root roses in frost-free shed; cover roots with damp straw/potting compost and sacks.	Firm bushes after strong wind.
Plant new, container-grown and bare-root shrubs.	Continue planting new bushes; refirm bushes after frost and wind.	Refirm bushes after frost and wind.
Plant new climbers and wall shrubs; tidy deciduous established ones after they have lost their leaves.	Plant new stock in fair weather. Check that ties are not too loose or too tight.	Check that ties are not too loose or too tight.
Plant new trees; prune existing ones to shape; remove dead and dying wood; dress young specimens with bone meal.	Continue pruning when no frost; check stakes and ties after wind; remove branches broken by wind or snow.	Check stakes and ties after wind; remove branches broken by wind or snow immediately.
Plant new conifers; tie up branches if falling out of shape.	Knock heavy snow off branches; firm in after wind.	Knock heavy snow off branches; firm in after wind.
Dig empty ground; harvest late crops; top raised beds with compost; sow peas and broad beans; plant onions, garlic.	Harvest winter crops; watch for bird damage on all overwintering plants; dig empty ground when fine.	Pick winter vegetables; dig empty ground when fine; plant shallots in new year; plan crops for next season.
Pick late apples and pears and store in boxes in a single layer; start pruning apples and pears for shape.	Continue pruning apples and pears; plant all top and soft fruit when milder.	Continue pruning in open weather; plant new trees and bushes.

Page references in *italic* indicate illustrations.

© RD = Reader's Digest Association, MW=Mark Winwood, SC=Sarah Cuttle
All artwork=© Reader's Digest Association

T=Top, B=Bottom, L=Left, R=Right, C=Centre

Cover Photolibrary.com/Ips Co Ltd, **1** Gap Photos Ltd/Visions, **2-3** The Garden Collection/Nicola Stocken Tomkin, **4** L The Garden Collection/Andrew Lawson, **4** C Gap Photos Ltd/Richard Bloom, **4** R Gap Photos Ltd/Lynn Keddie, **5** L The Garden Collection/Kevin Scully, **5** C Gap Photos Ltd/Richard Bloom, **5** R Gap Photos Ltd/Sharon Pearson, **6** Photolibrary.com/Mark Bolton, **8-9** The Garden Collection/Andrew Lawson, **11** Gap Photos Ltd/Visions, **13** Gap Photos Ltd/Clive Nichols, **14** T Gap Photos Ltd/Clare Matthews, **14** B Gap Photos Ltd/Julie King, **16** Gap Photos Ltd/Jerry Harpur, Design:Naila Green, **17** Cranfield University Soil Survey and Land Research Centre, **18** R Gap Photos Ltd/Visions, **18** BL Gap Photos Ltd/Lynn Keddie, **19** TL The Garden Collection/Andrew Lawson, **19** B Gap Photos Ltd/John Glover, **20** The Garden Collection/Nicola Stocken Tomkins, **21** Gap Photos Ltd/J S Sira.Design:Claire Whitehouse, **22** T The Garden Collection/Andrew Lawson, **22** B The Garden Collection/Derek St Romaine, **23** The Garden Collection/Jonathan Buckley, **24** The Garden Collection/Michelle Garrett, **25** L The Garden Collection/Jonathan Buckley, **25** R The Garden Collection/Andrew Lawson, **29** Gap Photos Ltd/Zara Napier, **30, 31** TL & TR © RD/MW, **31** BL The Garden Collection/Andrew Lawson, **33** T The Garden Collection/Derek Harris, **33** B The Garden Collection/Derek St Romaine, **34** © RD/MW, **35** The Garden Collection/Andrew Lawson, **36** iStockphoto.com/Pete Fleming, **37** © RD/MW, **38-39** © RD/SC, **40, 41** © RD/MW, **42** T The Garden Collection/Liz Eddison, **42** C © RD, **42** BL, BR © RD/MW, **43** © RD/SC, **44** L The Garden Collection/Gary Rogers, **44** R The Garden Collection/Nicola Stocken Tomkins, **45** © RD/MW, **46** The Garden Collection/Nicola Stocken Tomkins, **47** © RD/Mark Bolton, **49** © RD/MW, **50, 51** T&CL © RD, **51** BR, **52** © RD/SC, **53** © RD/MW, **54** © RD/SC, **55** TL, TR © RD/MW, **55** © RD, **56, 57, 58** © RD/MW, **59** T The Garden Collection/Derek St Romaine, **59** B The Garden Collection/Andrew Lawson, **60-61** Gap Photos Ltd/Lynn Keddie, **62** T © RD/SC, **62** BL, BR, **63, 64** TL, CL © RD/MW, **64** TR © RD/SC, **64** BR Gap Photos Ltd/Richard Bloom, **65** © RD/SC, **66** T Gap Photos Ltd/Visions, **66** B iStockphoto.com/Chad Truemper, **67** T Photolibrary.com/Mark Winwood, **67** B The Garden Collection/Gill Siddell, Peachings, **68-69** The Garden Collection/Kevin Scully, **70** The Garden Collection/Nicola Stocken Tomkins, **72** L Gap Photos Ltd/Howard Rice, **72** R The Garden Collection/Nicola Stocken Tomkins, **74** L, R © RD/SC, **74** C © RD, **75** TL, TC, TR © RD/MW, **75** B The Garden Collection/Jonathan Buckley, **76** The Garden Collection/Marie O'Hara, **77** © RD/SC, **78, 79** © RD/MW, **80** L Gap Photos Ltd/Rice/Buckland, **80** R The Garden Collection/Derek St Romaine, **81** T Photolibrary.com/Baker Maryellen, **81** BL Gap Photos Ltd/Paul Debois, **81** BR Gap Photos Ltd/Mark Bolton, **82** T Photolibrary.com/Howard Rice, **82** BL, BC, BR © RD/MW, **83** © RD/SC, **84** The Garden Collection/ Gary Rogers, **85** T Gap Photos Ltd/Sharon Pearson, **85** B Photolibrary.com/Sunniva Harte, **86, 87** © RD/SC, **88** T Gap Photos Ltd/J S Sira, **88** B The Garden Collection/Andrew Lawson, **89** TL, TC, TR © RD/SC, **89** BL, BR © RD/MW, **90** Gap Photos Ltd/Clive Nichols, **91** T Gap Photos Ltd/John Glover, **91** BL, CL, CR, BR © RD/MW, **92, 93** © RD/MW, **94** L The Garden Collection/Nicola Stocken Tomkins, **94** R The Garden Collection/Jane Sebire, **95** T The Garden Collection/Torie Chugg, **95** B The Garden Collection/Derek Harris, **96** The Garden Collection/Derek St Romaine, **97** L The Garden Collection/Liz Eddison, **97** R The Garden Collection/Neil Sutherland, **98-99** Gap Photos Ltd/Richard Bloom, **100, 101** © RD/SC **102** © RD/Debbie Patterson, **103, 105** © RD/SC, **106-107** Gap Photos Ltd/Sharon Pearson, **108** © RD/MW, **113** Gap Photos Ltd/S&O, **114** Gap Photos Ltd/Rice/Buckland, **116** L, CR, R Frank Lane Picture Agency/Nigel Cattlin, **116** CL The Garden Collection/Jonathan Buckley, **117** L, R Frank Lane Picture Agency/Nigel Cattlin, **117** CL Gap Photos Ltd/FhF Greenmedia, **117** CR Gap Photos Ltd/Claire Davies, **118** L Photolibrary.com/Howard Rice, **118** CL Photolibrary.com/Francois De Heel, **118** CR Gap Photos Ltd/Brian North, **118** R Photolibrary.com/Michael Howes, **119** L Photolibrary.com/Botanica, **119** CL, R Frank Lane Picture Agency/Nigel Cattlin, **119** CR Photolibrary.com/Sunniva Harte, **120** © RD/SC, **121** © RD/MW

Reader's Digest The First-time Gardener is based on material in *Reader's Digest All Seasons Guide to Gardening*; *Short Cuts to Great Gardens* and *New Encyclopedia of Garden Plants & Flowers*, all published by The Reader's Digest Association Limited, London.

First Edition Copyright © 2008

The Reader's Digest Association Limited,
11 Westferry Circus, Canary Wharf,
London E14 4HE **www.readersdigest.co.uk**

Editors John Andrews, Lisa Thomas
Art Editor Jane McKenna
Consultant and writer Daphne Ledward-Hands
Proofreader Barry Gage
Indexer Vanessa Bird

Reader's Digest General Books
Editorial Director Julian Browne
Art Director Anne-Marie Bulat
Managing Editor Nina Hathway
Head of Book Development Sarah Bloxham
Picture Resource Manager Sarah Stewart-Richardson
Pre-press Account Manager Dean Russell
Production Controller Sandra Fuller
Product Production Manager Claudette Bramble

Origination Colour Systems Limited, London
Printed in China

We are committed both to the quality of our products and the service we provide to our customers. We value your comments, so please do contact us on **08705 113366** or via our website at **www.readersdigest.co.uk**

If you have any comments or suggestions about the content of our books, email us at **gbeditorial@readersdigest.co.uk**

ISBN 978 0 276 44268 1
BOOK CODE 400-369 UP0000-1
ORACLE CODE 250011974H.00.24